Dedicated to the memory of my Dad,
GEORGE CAMP 1898-1986

ROOTS
IN THE
ROCKIES

FRANK CAMP

To Mary-Ann & Jim

Edie Camp

July 28, 1997

FRANK CAMP VENTURES
Box 165,
Ucluelet, B.C.
V0R 3A0

PRINTING HISTORY
First printing – June 1993

PRODUCTION CREDITS
Typesetting – Sunfire Publications, Langley, B.C.
Design & Layout – Garnet Basque
Printing – Colorcraft Limited, Hong Kong

PHOTO CREDITS
Front cover – Ted Panos - Emily Holmes
Back cover – Arvon Hilworth
Permission to use map – Ted Hart

CANADIAN CATALOGUING IN PUBLICATION DATA

Camp, Frank, 1926 -
    Roots in the Rockies

ISBN 0-9697015-0-0

    1. Camp, Frank, 1926 -   2. Park rangers —
Alberta—Biography. 3. Canadian Parks Service—
Officials and employees—Biography. 4. National
parks and reserves—Alberta—History.
I. Title.
SB481.6.C34A3 1993   333.78'3'092   C93-091281-0

To my wife, Edie
Like her mother, a woman of
great strength and courage.

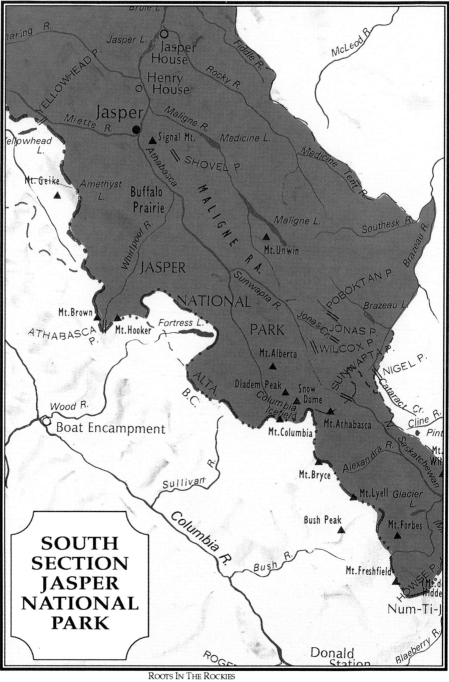

SOUTH SECTION JASPER NATIONAL PARK

CONTENTS

The author, 1927, in front of the cabin where he was born. Grandma Maryanne Camp seated with Mom Louise Camp standing.

INTRODUCTION

MY dad, George Camp migrated from England to Alberta in 1912 and helped my grandfather open up a quarter section of bushland for a homestead north west of Edmonton. In 1918 Dad moved to the Rockies. After working at a variety of jobs he decided to make a career of packer, guide or cook working for many of the first outfitters and guides based in Jasper. His first employer was Fred Brewster. In 1940 he became a Park Warden for Jasper National Park and held this position until he retired.

In 1924 he married my mother, Marie Louise Perreault and moved back to the homestead hoping to make a success as a farmer. I was born on the homestead in 1926 and my sister was born in 1929 in the small community of Vimy, where Dad had moved looking for work. The great depression was on and nearly everyone on the prairies was on the brink of starvation with no opportunity to work.

Hoping conditions would be better in the mountains, Dad moved the family back to Jasper in 1930 and found work in a Relief Camp. As a boy of five years of age, I remember clearly many of the events that followed our arrival. Our first home was a shack in the town-site but we soon moved to a small three room cabin in the Otto Brothers corrals.

Listening to the men who travelled the mountains relating their adventures and experiences made me dream that someday I would have the same opportunity to live this way of life. As soon as I learned to ride a horse, I often travelled with Dad. As I grew older I spent most of my free time exploring the mountains around Jasper.

World War II interrupted this lifestyle for the two years I was in the Navy. When I returned I still had the urge to work in the back country with horses and I was fortunate to be employed as a Park Warden.

The experience I had growing up at a time when many of the early travellers of the Rocky Mountains were still around and my association with the National Park Service has given me the impulse to write about my life and my family living in the Rocky Mountains.

1

IN THE FOOTSTEPS
OF THE FUR TRADERS

IT was the spring of 1946, the war was over and I had returned to my home in Jasper. Two years before at the age of 17, I had quit school, hopped a freight to Edmonton and joined the Navy. Why, I'm not sure, having not seen the ocean, but I guess I thought it was a great way to see the world. Within about 6 months I was a trained torpedoman and posted to the frigate HMCS Poundmaker operating out of St. John's Newfoundland on North Atlantic convoy patrol. These were the dying days of the U Boat wolf packs in their final attempt to stop supplies from reaching the war front. My action station was on the quarterdeck dropping depth charges when echo soundings indicated a submarine nearby. Once I had overcome my initial sea-sickness I found life on the ocean adventurous and exciting. When V.E. day came in May of 1945 the Navy turned its attention to the South Pacific and asked for volunteers. I signed up hoping to go but the war with Japan soon ended and everything changed.

The return to civilian life without a plan for the future found most of the veterans sitting around beer tables reminiscing about the past and speculating about the future. The community of Jasper had two stable economies, railroading and National Parks. Most of my associates were horsemen and mountain men, many who had served with the Rocky Mountain Rangers. For most of us it seemed natural to apply for positions with the Park Service as packers, blacksmiths, trail and cabin builders, or Park Wardens.

I thought my chances to qualify as a Park Warden were good, especially having travelled with my Dad who was a Park Warden and had taken me with him during the summer holidays on his patrols. I made application for the job and was successful.

As an introduction to the work I was sent with Dad to the headwaters of the Whirlpool River. It was late spring and the snow in the high country had not begun to melt. The first stop was a cabin called the Tie Camp located at the site of an old abandoned logging camp that housed a large crew of railroad tie-hackers during the construction of the railroad prior to the first world war.

In the spring when the river broke up the ties were rafted down the Whirlpool River into the Athabasca and down the Athabasca to a location adjacent to the present day airfield and taken ashore with a device called a jackladder. The Otto Brothers, Jack, Bruce and Closson were the contractors who supplied most of the ties for the railroad. Until sometime in the late 40's or early 50's, a cabin called Otto's

(Right) The author as a new recruit to the National Parks Warden Service in 1946. (Below) Simon Creek cabin, built by George Camp in 1945.

Cache, stood near the Valley of the Crooked Trees and was used as a way-station for moving supplies and equipment between Jasper and the Tie Camps.

The next stop up-river was Simon Creek where Dad had constructed a small cabin the previous year. We laid over for a day to build some furniture and put in a stove. Our next move was to the cabin on the Middle Fork of the Whirlpool. Although the cabin was the best constructed of all the shelters on the Whirlpool River, its location was the poorest. Built on the gravel bed of the river it was subject to flood and soil erosion in high water. There was no horse feed near the cabin and really no reason to stop over except in winter. Some thought to build here initially must have been the possibility of using the cabin as a base camp to patrol the headwaters of the Middle Fork and Whirlpool Pass. The Park Boundary was along the continental divide at this point giving poachers access from the Canoe River watershed in B.C. From the Middle Fork cabin the trail returns to the main river and passes through a swamp spruce forest. At this point Dad drew my attention to an old trail blaze registry. Faintly outlined was the name G. Franchere 1814 which was a sure sign we were on the trail first explored as a possible fur trade route by David Thompson.

David Thompson started his career as a clerk for the Hudson Bay company in 1784 in eastern Canada and soon became a successful trader. In 1790 he studied surveying and map-making and developed an exceptional skill in the application of this knowledge. Soon recognized by company officials he was assigned the task of seeking a direct route from the Hudson Bay to Lake Athabasca.

In 1797 he left the service of the Hudson Bay Company and accepted a position with the North West Company (N.W.C.). His assignment was to locate and map all N.W.C posts east of the Rockies. Thompson then moved on to open trade with the Indians west of the Rockies. In 1807 he ascended the North Saskatchewan River from Rocky Mountain House to the mouth of the Howse River, up the Howse and over the continental divide, down the Blaeberry River and into the Columbia River Basin to Kootenay House.

In 1810 on a return trip to the Columbia he was stopped by the Indians from using Howse Pass. With the help of another trader, Alexander Henry, an alternate route up the Athabasca River was explored. Leaving the Saskatchewan River they travelled north to Chip Lake, then westerly until they reached the Athabasca River near Obed. Somewhere near the north end of Brule Lake they set up a permanent camp and remained there for over three weeks. Seven men with horses were sent back to Rocky

Mountain House with a request to return with additional supplies. Reaching Rocky Mt. House, the relief party was told that no provisions were available.

In the meantime Thompson continued up the Athabasca and Whirlpool Rivers, crossed the divide and reached the Canoe River where it enters the Columbia River. At this site, known as the Boat Encampment, Thompson and his men built an 25' boat and ascended the Columbia River to its headwaters. Crossing overland at Canal Flats he descended the Kootenay River returning to the lower section of the Columbia River and continued on to tide water. Thompson's objective was to establish a trading post at the mouth of the Columbia but the Pacific Fur Company had arrived from New York on the sailing vessel, the Tonquin, owned by John Jacob Astor, and built Fort Astoria.

The Tonquin continued up the coast to trade with the Indians and one of its stop-overs was near the present village of Tofino on the west coast of Vancouver Island. The Captain, noted for his brashness and brutality, annoyed the Indians who attacked the ship killing all but five of the crew who escaped in an open boat but were soon caught and also killed. The following day when the Indians again boarded the vessel, it exploded with a tremendous blast killing nearly everyone. It is speculated that a lone survivor had hidden in the ship's magazine and before being found had ignited the gun powder.

Later, as a result of the War of 1812, Fort Astoria was transferred into Canadian hands in the guise of the N.W.C. and was immediately re-named Fort George.

Now referring back to the blazed tree register on the Whirlpool River. Gabriel Franchere had arrived at Fort Astoria via the Tonquin as a clerk for John Jacob Astor.

When the N.W.C. took possession of the fort and re-named it Fort George, Franchere refused to accept a position with the Canadian company and was allowed to return east by way of the Athabasca Pass route. Franchere's account of the trip through the mountains has been written up in a publication titled, "Voyage to the North West Coast of America", Gabriel Franchere 1811-14 graphically describes his journey. Of interest was Franchere's note of the buffalo carcasses that he saw soon after leaving the mouth of the Whirlpool and crossing the Athabasca River. Unfortunately I did not appreciate the significance of the tree registry at the time.

Our next night on the trail was spent in a teepee at the foot of Athabasca Pass at a site Dad called Kane Meadows. The foot of Mt. Kane was to our east. Across the river from our campsite was the remains of an old log structure that was thought to be the site

Kane Meadows Teepee - Spring, 1946.

of Camp de Fusil. The history of this site remains a mystery to me to this day. Our teepee had been set up in the fall and by the time we arrived the winter snows had buried the skirt cutting off ventilation. We cooked our evening meal over a very smoky fire and soon rolled in to sleep with the fire still smouldering. I awoke to a loud noise and saw the shadow form of Dad doubled up in pain and retching uncontrollably. In a few moments he became violently ill and then complete silence. I was sure he had passed out and I was at a loss to know what to do. After a while he was able to crawl back into his sleeping bag and ensure me he thought he would be alright. It may have been the smoke or the re-heated stew that we had for supper. It was common practise to cook a large stew and let the leftover freeze. Usually the stew pot was hung up in the cabin and remained frozen until the next patrol.

I was reminded of a previous incident when Dad and his partner Curly Phillips were trapping on the Hay and Berland Rivers north west of Hinton. It was during the depression in the winter of 1936 when the price of a squirrel pelt brought five cents. In order to cover as much territory to trap, Dad and Curly separated and on a pre-determined day met at a certain trapper's cabin to exchange information. At this one meeting the stew pot was hanging on the ridge pole half full of frozen stew and was soon taken down and placed over the fire. Darkness came early and dining was by candle light. Both men had a generous helping, leaving a small morsel in the pot. Curly commented that he was full so Dad thought he would clean it up. As he tipped the pot over his plate, the largest most well-stewed mouse slid over the lip of the pot and landed with a splat on the plate. The obvi-

Athabasca Pass Tent Shelter

ous lesson was put a lid on the pot next time.

In the morning, after a poor night's sleep, the best solution to the smoke problem was to move on although Dad was not too steady on his feet. The next stop was to be at timberline at the foot of Athabasca Pass. A small tent spread over a pole frame had been left as a shelter. The problem was to find it in the deep snow. Dad knew the general location but all there was to indicate where, was a mound of snow above the normal level snowpack. After a few false digs using a snowshoe for a shovel the tent was found. A rusty air-tight heater was a welcome sight and after clearing the snow from the top of the tent, we pushed a stove pipe up through and got a fire started. The next day was a lay-over and a short climb into the Pass gave us a great view of the Hooker Icefield and Kane Glacier. We returned to the tent for the night and with an early start travelled back to the Middlefork cabin. Two days later we were back at the highway and on into Jasper. A story of interest that Dad related to me during this patrol was about a lost gold deposit just over Athabasca Pass on Jeffrey Creek. When descending from the Pass to the Wood River the first stream crossed is Pacific Creek and soon after, Jeffrey Creek. The trail follows Jeffrey Creek for a short distance before it reached the Wood River. The story so often told by the old-timers is that sometime after the turn of the century a prospector struck it rich and found an unbelievable gold deposit. As winter approached he returned to his base in Golden, B.C. carrying a large amount of the gold. During the winter he became ill and eventually died. Before he died he took his nephew into his confidence and told him the location of the strike and of the fact that he had left a much larger amount of gold buried under the floor of the tent. He had left, expecting to return the following spring to retrieve the cache. As the story unfolds, the nephew returned to the site on Jeffrey creek and in vain could not locate the camp-site. Winter avalanches and spring mudslides had changed the face of the valley floor and it was impossible to relate the terrain to the map.

The Otto Brothers, famous for their ability as guides and out-fitters lived in Golden at this time and for years after the news was out, returned each summer to the site hoping to find its loca-tion. In 1935 a mining syndicate from eastern Canada arrived in Jasper with 12 men who were geologists or prospectors. The exact time and details of the event are hard to determine but Dad had pictures of some of the incidence that took place. They hired a pack outfit, and after trucking their equipment and supplies to the bridge over the Whirlpool River, started moving this large amount of goods by packhorses up the Whirlpool, over Athabas-ca Pass and down to Jeffrey Creek and established a base camp. Dad was hired as a packer during this time and most of the sum-mer was spent freighting into the camp. The object of the exercise was to find the missing gold. The effort this expedition put into the search would certainly lead one to believe the story was real. In the fall the project was abandoned and the camp moved out down the Columbia River with no local knowledge of the out-come of their efforts.

CHAPTER

HORSES – ESSENTIAL FOR THE BACK COUNTRY TRAVELLER

R ETURNING to the Jasper valley, spring was in the air and my anticipation was to be assigned to my own district but the Chief Warden had other plans.

My assignment was to work with the Barn-boss, "Happy" Riley to round up the Warden Service horses that had been on the winter range. With few exceptions over one hundred horses were put out to winter pasture in two locations. One area was called the Maligne range along the east side of the Athabasca downstream from the mouth of the Maligne River and the Buffalo Prairie range on the east side of the Athabasca south of Jasper.

I enjoyed this work because I was very familiar with the area and horses. When our family returned to Jasper in 1930 after starving out on the homestead northwest of Edmonton we lived in a shingle-sided shack in the east end of the village. Dad soon found a small frame building located in the Otto Brothers corral adjacent to the National Park horse corrals and barns. We lived at that location for five years while Dad worked as a packer and trail hand with anyone of the number of outfitters who were located along the Pyramid Lake road. Guiding and Outfitting was big business at that time and some of the old-timers who operated from this area included the Otto Brothers, Curly Phillips, Jack Hargreaves, Stan Kitchen, Red

Home in Otto's Corral, 1933. Myself, Grandad Camp, sister Maryanne, and Mom.

Creighton and Brewsters. During the peak of this activity over 500 head of horses grazed on open range east of Jasper town-site.

Growing up in this environment was a hands on experience with horses and cowboys and at an early age I had a fair knowledge of horses. When the horses were brought in from the winter range they were usually in poor shape and some had to be barn fed for days before they could be put to work. As kids we could earn five cents for each beer bottle of wood ticks we could pick off a horse.

Although the outfitters headquartered in the Park, most of trail trips went to outlying areas beyond the Park boundary, for example, all hunting trips. It was always a bonus hanging out at the stables when you were allowed to travel with the guides trailing the horses to a trail head where the party was to start their trip.

Our home in the corrals came to a sudden end for me when coming home for lunch from school one day, all that was left was the outhouse. I suppose my parents had mentioned it to me that we were moving but who would have expected the house to go too. Jack Otto had decided to relocate the building on a foundation in the town-site at the corner of Bonhomme and Aspen Street. It was a fairly easy task to lift the building up and by taking two wagons and extending the reach that ran between the front and back wheels, lowered the structure on to the wagons. Two teams of mules provided the power and when I caught up to my lunch it was nearing the site where it still sits on to this day.

I remember how impressed I was with indoor plumbing, electric lights and hot water from a tap. My greatest fear was flushing the toilet as I was sure the rush of water would keep flowing until the bowl overflowed. For the longest time I would never exceed three squares of toilet paper in case I plugged up the system. This concern had also been influenced by my mother's extreme austerity program as these were the days of the great depression when maximum utilization of everything was necessary for survival.

Our first winter in our new home was cold. An extension to provide kitchen space and the basement were unfinished, and Mom spent most of her time keeping a small heater going. Dad was on the trapline with Curly Phillips but made it home just before Christmas. In the fall when he was preparing to go trapping, he had borrowed $14.00 from someone to buy a single shot .22 rifle, some shells and a slab of bacon expecting to repay the money from the sale of his furs at Christmas time. The day of his homecoming is still very vivid in my mind. His Trapper Nelson pack was loaded with squirrel pelts with average pelts selling for five cents, above average worth ten cents and prime—the unbelievable price of fifteen cents! He dropped his pack in the basement and came upstairs where Mom, my sister, Maryanne and I sat with him in the kitchen to hear him tell us about his trip. Naturally the question was how much money would we have for Christmas from the sale of his fur.

Our pet dog, a small terrier we called Buster was also caught up in the excitement but we were paying little attention to him and didn't realize he was no longer in the kitchen. After the initial welcome home, Dad took me into the basement to let me help him unpack and to our astonishment and utter dismay found Buster tearing the pack apart and tossing pelts all over the room! Why Buster didn't become history at that moment I don't know. Many of the pelts had been punctured which down-graded them to minimum value and Christmas wasn't as great as expected.

Curly Phillips was a visionary who could see the potential of the tourist trade to the Rockies and by 1936 had proven his point. His camp at Maligne Lake flourished, pack trips into remote areas of the Rockies and canoe trips on the major waterways all contributed to the recognition he received from many famous travellers the world over. The 1932 Winter Olympics at Lake Placid had started a trend that began to spread across America and Curly knew someday that the Jasper area would be famous as a ski resort. He built a lodge in Shangri-La that for years afterwards was used as a shelter for skiers in the Watchtower Basin.

After Christmas in 1936 Dad and Curly took me and his three kids winter camping up a trail he had cut to timberline on Signal Mtn. It was about a six-mile run down to the road at Maligne Canyon. When descending, with ski-poles dragging from our wrists, each of us was given a small tree about five feet long with all but the last two feet cleared of limbs. Because of our limited skiing ability, especially in turning we had the choice of placing it between our legs or to one side or the other for turning corners. The harder you pushed down the more control you had. New Year's Eve was clear and cold and as we lay in our sleeping bags we heard the steam-train whistles down below us ringing in the New Year.

The Curly Phillips Guiding and Outfitting continued to operate with the help of his brother Harry and Curly's wife, Grace. Dad worked at the chalet at Maligne Lake in the summer. Sam, Curly's and Grace's son, and I enjoyed the privilege of having the run of the place. Our time was spent fishing, boating, and hiking wherever our fancy took us.

This came to a sudden end on September 1, 1939 when we returned to camp in the evening. Dad had heard that Hitler had invaded Poland and war was declared. Wes Merrill was the horse wrangler at the camp and he thought he had better head for town, get his rifle and go join the fight. Dad asked him if he would take us kids to town with him. For years after, I would occasionally hear that Wes was still in the army after surviving the hazards of the war. Soon after, the business was sold. Harry Phillips, having survived a grizzly bear attack that had bitten off one of his fingers when he had shoved his hat in the bear's mouth to keep from being bitten, died from a "widow-maker" when the top of a tree came down hitting him on the head while cutting poles for a bridge.

In 1940 Dad joined the Park Warden Service and was posted to the Rocky River District, replacing Ed McDonald, who had been the warden on this district for years, but recently had been injured when surprised by a grizzly and bucked off his horse. On one of my trips with Dad we passed the site of the accident and Dad briefly commented on what happened. Later I visited Ed at his cabin at Pyramid Lake and he provided more details.

He had just left the Grizzly cabin which is the half way shelter between the Rocky and Jacques lake and had travelled about a mile when he sur-

Park Warden George Camp

prised a grizzly feeding on buffalo berries (soapolallie). His horse reared, unloaded him and took off. Fortunately the bear also took off leaving Ed on the trail with what later proved to be a broken pelvis. Unable to walk, he crawled on his stomach back to the Grizzly cabin. The accident happened on the edge of the first dry wash west of the cabin and just a short distance away was an old shelter probably used by Ed before the present cabin was built. He made it to this old shelter and if I recall correctly, stayed overnight lying on the ground. His next effort was to make it to the Grizzly cabin.

On his arrival he had great difficulty in getting the door open and once inside even greater difficulty trying to reach the telephone nailed high on the wall. The phone was the old forestry type with the hand crank and separate receiver. His first effort was to knock the receiver off the hook, opening the transmitter circuit and lying on his back, hollering from a distance hoping someone on the line would hear him. This did not work out so he had to improvise a way of lifting himself up to be able to ring and alert Charlie Matheson, the warden at Maligne Lake. He eventually accomplished this task and a rescue party was sent out from Jasper. The rescue party led by Warden Frank Wells carried Ed to Jasper on a stretcher suspended between two horses.

When Ed recovered from his ordeal he was transferred to the Maligne Lake district and retired at the end of the war after a long and interesting career.

Ed was the district warden of the Rocky River in the '30's and probably even before that time. His original headquarters cabin was on the Medicine Tent River five miles up river from the present Rocky Forks cabin at the foot of Deception Pass. The reason the cabin was located there was access to the coal mining town of Mountain Park which was one of many boom towns that comprised the area known as the "coal branch". The C.N.R. served this area with a branch line from Edson, Alberta. He patrolled east to Cairn Pass, down the Southesk River and up the Brazeau to Nigel Pass.

In later years I confirmed this information when I patrolled this area. Ed used to build split log teepees chinked with moss and the three I located were, one on the Brazeau between Isaac Creek cabin and the Dowling ford, one near the present Isaac Creek cabin and one on a branch of the Brazeau that drains the southeast basin below Jonas Shoulder about a mile from the present Four Point cabin.

One of Ed MacDonald's split pole teepees.

As a pastime when stopping at one of Ed's old cabin sites I would search out small hidden caches that Ed habitually put out. Many of the items were of little value but were always neatly packaged. My greatest anticipation was to locate a tobacco can full of money but this never happened.

My last personal contact with Ed was at Pyramid Lake in the winter of 1948 when the wardens were on a predator control program killing wolves. We had left two dead wolves on the island at Pyramid and on the way home had stopped to have coffee with Ed. I told him of the wolves and he asked if he could go and take the heads off as he wanted to save the skulls. I told him to go ahead, which he did but I never followed up on what he did with them.

In the summer of 1942 as a summer student, I had worked for the National Parks building a trail up the Astoria River from Cavell Lake to the Tonquin Valley. The previous year the trail crew had completed the trail to what later became the site of the Old Horn cabin. The Park provided tools and tents and we had to provision ourselves. Our cook was an old-timer who had spent most of his life in the North, subsisting on sourdough. The menu never varied, sourdough bread, biscuits or pancakes, canned sausages, eggs, potatoes boiled or fried, canned peas and dried fruit served in a variety of combinations. Canned milk, tea, coffee, sugar and jam helped round out the diet. The trail boss was Bruce Otto, one of the famous Otto brothers.

Bruce was a renowned mountain man with tales to tell that were spell-binding. Most of his stories had an element of truth and some exaggeration but always plausible. Years before he had guided James Oliver Curwood on a grizzly hunt that had all the excitement expected of a bear hunt. A book written by Curwood following this hunt gives Bruce credit for the success of the hunt and named the book "The Grizzly King", first published in 1915. The hunt changed Curwood's lust for the kill to one of compassion for wild animals. The movie released in 1988 called "The Bear" gives a dramatized version of the book and the actual hunt. A lot of the actual filming took place in the Rockies.

The next summer, 1943, I decided to be a real cowboy and hired out to Jack Hargreaves to operate his pony barn. We first had to find and corral the horses that were scattered along the Athabasca Valley from Jasper to the Green Timber near Brule Lake.

Many of the horses had been running wild during the war years and young stallions had the run of the range. We had a horse trap just southeast of Fiddle River against a rock cliff and a corral with a drift fence near Pocahontas that had belonged to an old outfitter Ralph James. We would ride out from our camp in the morning looking for tracks and if lucky find some horses. Half the time Jack wasn't too sure if they were his or not but we would start them back to the corral and sometimes be lucky enough to catch a few.

Jack was another of these old-timers who you were never sure if everything he said was gospel. One of his favourite tricks was to pick out a saddle horse for you to ride expounding on the great virtues of the animal, but as soon as you had saddled and mounted up, were immediately bucked off. With his high pitched laugh and shaking his head he would state he must have the wrong horse.

After a few hard days of riding we came home with 22 head of horses that could be ridden. During that summer troop trains of American soldiers passed through Jasper enroute to the Alaska Highway or to Haines, Alaska. There was a six-hour layover and my job was to encourage the soldiers to go for a ride. The cost was $2.00 a ride and double if they were brought back lathered. In the evening the horses were turned loose to graze up around Pyramid Lake and at 4 o'clock the next morning I had to go and find them. You never lost your horses but there were times you didn't get back to the stables and breakfast until noon. Jack kept a stallion in the barn to use as a "jingle" horse and when you gave him his head in the morning to search out the horses you got the ride of your life. Returning to the corrals with the herd ahead of you was even a greater test of skill just to be kept from getting knocked from the saddle as old "Smoky" tried to overtake the horses ahead of him.

In the fall, Jack needed a cook for a hunting party. My summer's wages were $2 a day and with a promise of $4 a day I thought I could handle the job. The guide was Frank Moberly and we had one hunter. With twelve pack horses our first day's travel was up the Snake Indian River to Shale Banks where we camped for the night.

Not only was I a poor cook but had never set up a pyramid cook tent. I served supper that night using the tent as a ground sheet to the disgust of the guide and dismay of the hunter. My next problem was packing. The guide helped me break camp in the morning and pack the horses. He rode in the lead with the hunter and I hazed the pack horses ahead of me. When a pack began to look like it was coming loose or might roll, my job was to catch that horse and make the adjustment.

The rest of the outfit continued up the trail and the horse I had held back became excited thinking he would be left behind. Once turned loose he would gallop flat out to catch up scaring the rest of the horses and more often than not, upset another pack. The whole performance was repeated again and again and all I got from Moberly was a look of disdain. Needless to say I soon became an expert packer and before the trip was over, when I packed up in the morning the pack stayed put until we made camp.

Returning to school late after an adventurous summer made my adjustment to the school routine dull and it was soon after Christmas that the Navy looked like the way to go.

Two years later I'm working with Happy Riley rounding up the Park horses off the winter range and helping the blacksmith shoe the horses that would be going out to the various warden districts.

Most wardens were very possessive of the horses they had worked in previous summers and if the barn boss wanted to make any changes he was usually met with great opposition. One of the problems was, as the horses grew old and new stock was brought in, the wardens knew they could expect trouble working with unfamiliar stock, especially keeping them from continually wanting to pull out of unfamiliar grazing sites on the districts.

An outbreak of sleeping sickness was another problem. A veterinarian, Dr. Love, from Elk Island National Park was called to Jasper to help us test each horse. A blood sample was taken from the jugular vein into a test tube and within minutes, if there was a distinct separation of the red blood and plasma, the test was positive and the horse destroyed.

With the horses reduced in number and the replacement program on hold during the war, it was necessary to bring the herd up to the working number by purchasing from an outside source. Charlie Phillips and Dad went out to the prairies to the district of Sundre and contacted a rancher, Dave McMurtry, who had a general idea of the type of horse the Park needed. Charlie Phillips and Dad travelled about the country with McMurtry, visiting farms and ranches until they had selected about 60 head. All shapes, sizes, colours, ages, dispositions and training were included in the package and trailed over the mountains to Jasper. The horses were pushed hard and alternately ridden on the trip so when they arrived in Jasper they appeared to be well broke and easily handled which many of them were—but as in any horse deal "buyer beware."

Each warden was expected to take one or two of the horses and work them with his regular string. There were many horror stories that came back from the wardens on the behaviour of some of the horses, but it was not always the horses' fault. Some of the new warden recruits were as green as the horses and the first rule when working with horses is "you gotta be smarter than the horse". A sign in the Chief Warden's Office stated, "Don't call us if you lose your horses, we don't have them here."

A patrol to the Tonquin Valley came next. Dad had asked for assistance to pack into the Old Horn cabin a double-tiered bunk

*Snowball - The indispensable pack horse climbing from the headwaters of the
Brazeau River over Nigel Pass.*

bed. The bed consisted of two single spring frames and two
uprights for the legs and when assembled provide two comfortable cots for the small cabin. We left the trail head at Cavell Lake
with each a spring and an upright on our backs tied to a Trapper
Nelson backboard. Snow was melting on the trail and too wet to
snowshoe so we travelled on foot with the bottom of our packs
often dropping in the snow.

It is about six miles from the trail head to the cabin and we
arrived at our destination in early afternoon. The first thought
was to drop our packs and boil the tea pail. Taking our packs off
we both experienced the strangest sensation. All during the trip
the cot springs had a rhythmic movement back and forth and as
we walked our bodies had become so conditioned to this back
and forth action, that when the packs were dropped we continued to uncontrollably move back and forth for some time after-
ward. We found it rather entertaining trying to prepare lunch
going through this muscular spasm but eventually things
returned to normal.

Our next thought was, let's assemble this bunk bed and have
a rest. To our dismay we had packed in two springs from one
model of bed and two uprights from another style and they
wouldn't fit! Discouraged and annoyed with ourselves we put the
springs on blocks of wood and rested. It wasn't until sometime
later that Dad packed in a hand drill and very tediously drilled
holes and bolted the bunks together.

3

BEAR MANAGEMENT POLICY: SHOOT TO KILL

THE administration of the Park in those early days was definitely autocratic. The Superintendent was supreme and his managers well aware of his expectations. Hiring or firing or management problems requiring a decision stopped at the Superintendent's office. Game management was no exception and problems were solved on the spot. Many of these decisions had long lasting negative results necessitating the development of a Policy and Planning statement for Park use.

Taxpayers were demanding justification from the government for setting aside such a large tract of land for a park with very limited commercial development opportunity. The Canadian National Railroad passes through the park and soon public pressure demanded some concessions for tourist development. Land was leased for the building of facilities including the Jasper Park Lodge. Visitors were encouraged to come to the area to take in the beauty of the mountains from their parlour cars, tour busses or the comfort of exclusive accommodation. The expectation was that wild animals could be viewed close at hand at any time. To ensure these expectations were met, the park supported various programs that once introduced became difficult to control.

Historically there were elk herds in the Athabasca valley but for reasons undetermined there were no elk at the time of this accelerated park use. To correct this, 100 elk were shipped from Yellowstone in 1928-29 to Jasper by rail. Only two animals did not survive the trip and the other 98 were turned loose near the Jasper Railroad station. For the next two winters they were fed hay to encourage them to stay in the area. Within twelve years there were over 1000 elk in the valley and feed became scarce.

Heavy browsing took place so the Park had to begin a herd reduction program trying to kill a number of elk equal to the anticipated annual calf crop. As many as 700 elk were slaughtered in one season. Naturally public opinion was strong against this program. Hunters wanted the right to hunt in the park and visitors and animal protection activists were appalled at the slaughter. The elk were over-grazing and starving themselves to the extent that they had to forage by eating the bark off the aspen trees. If no control was taken, a mass die-off from starvation was expected.

One of the greatest attractions to visit the park was to see the bears and very few people were disappointed. Garbage dumps were maintained at many resorts and they came to feed giving visitors an excellent opportunity to observe and take pictures. First the black bears discovered this handout but it wasn't long before the more cautious grizzly also frequented these feeding grounds, much to the delight of the visitor. Before bears discovered the succulent tid-bits of a garbage feeding station they considered man a danger but as new generations of bears accepted handouts they took an offensive role and became dangerous.

Bear attacks on people became more frequent and once again the Park had to take positive action. The first approach was to shoot the bear. When the Jasper Park Lodge closed for a few years during the war, the bears moved into the town of Jasper. At least 60 black bears were shot at this time by the wardens.

After helping with the spring roundup I was assigned to a number of other tasks before I got a posting to the Brazeau River District. The exact chronological sequence of these tasks I cannot verify.

A request to the Park Office for my old diaries and summaries prior to 1950 resulted in a reply that prior to 1950 all this information was destroyed. I recall this information being stored in the far recesses of the attic in what is now the National Parks Information Centre. My request for Dad's diaries brought the same answer but I did receive both my diaries and Dad's beginning in the 50's. I am in possession of Dad's journals going back to 1952 and also my own journals for that period of time. Over the years I've collected hundreds of pictures going back to my Grandfather's time that complement everything that is covered by this story. Most of these pictures are not dated or titled but I'm familiar with the events they depict.

For the first few years after the war the general attitude towards any steady employment or long-term planning was "What the hell". Once I transferred to the Brazeau a registration book kept at the Waterfalls cabin my had an accurate account of travels to and from the Brazeau River district. Registrations went back to 1929 and were a priceless record of the traffic that passed by. Original sketches of the famous western cartoonist, Stu Cameron, from Calgary were always entertaining to view. The book has since been removed and I hope it surfaces somewhere for archival purposes.

I was sent to the Rocky River District with Jack Christiansen to shoot grizzlies. We were equipped with the 1895 Lee Enfield saddle carbine .303 and war surplus ammunition. The tips of the slugs had to be cut-off to keep the bullets from passing right through the animals. The decision to reduce the grizzly population was justified because for years the Rocky River district was without a District Warden and the bears had taken over the territory. The cabins had been ransacked, windows knocked out and doors ripped off. The corners of the cabins were used as rubbing posts and the bears had absolutely no fear of humans or horses.

On our first trip in to the district, the snow was still on the trail and we had to backpack the supplies we needed. Within a few days we had shot three grizzly on Osborne Creek and concluded it would be better to set a bait as there were still many tracks. Returning to town we obtained an old horse, bought more supplies and returned to the Jacques Lake cabin. Shooting the horse, we set a bait in Osborne Creek

One of the many grizzly bears shot on the Rocky River District in the spring of 1946.

secured to a large tree and waited. We checked the bait frequently and soon had three more grizzly.

One morning a phone call over the forestry phone from the caretaker reported a grizzly trying to break into the Brewster chalet at Maligne Lake asking for help. I said I would go and Jack would stay at Jacques Lake to watch the bait. That afternoon I hiked out to the Beaver cabin and caught a ride over the fire access road to Maligne. Next morning I crossed a grizzly track leaving the lake shore near the chalet and followed it into the Opal Hills. By mid-afternoon, following the timberline I spotted the bear sunning himself beside a rock near a small patch of scrub alpine fir. There was very little cover to keep out of sight but the wind was in my favour. I really didn't want to get too close in case my first shot didn't count and he could put the run on me. I finally was satisfied that I could get a good shot away and pulled down on him. I hit him behind the front shoulder but the old army ammunition just wasn't enough to keep him down. Off he went into the small patch of alpine fir and for about a half hour he thrashed about, then all was quiet. I sat around until dusk not daring to crawl into the brush but wanting to be sure he was finished.

I returned to Jacques Lake next morning and while Jack and I had lunch he told me about his experience during the night. The previous evening he had walked down to the creek and caught a couple of fair size dolly varden, cleaned them and hung them high on a pole in front of the cabin. He woke up during he night to the sound of two grizzlies standing on their hind legs fighting and trying to reach the fish. He opened the door and shot one and the other took off. In the morning he got up at daylight to go and check the bait and had to step over the one lying dead in the yard. There was a black bear on the bait so he shot it and returned to the cabin for breakfast. To his surprise the bear he had stepped over in the morning was gone.

"Well at least after lunch we can go up to the bait and check out the black bear," he commented. To our surprise the black bear was also gone. By now we were a little concerned about what was going on but after a search around the bait found a trail going off into the bush appearing as if something had been dragged. In about 300 yards a large circular area of ground had been pulled to the centre in a mound and buried underneath was the black bear. We knew for sure we had another grizzly around and increased our watch on the bait. There was a lot of speculation about the size of this unseen bear and in a couple of days we were not disappointed when he paid us a visit. We watched as he came into view and when he approached the bait broadsides to us, we both shot and down he went. A couple of extra shots to the front legs ensured us he wouldn't go anywhere. Our instructions were to shoot and destroy as many bears as we found but not to try and save the hides. When we checked this one out he was a prime bear 9 feet 3 inches from his nose to his tail and an excellent pelt.

Without hesitation or a projected plan of what we could do with the hide, we skinned the bear. Packing it back to the cabin was hot and heavy work. It was mid-day and the warm spring sun was bringing out clouds of flies. We knew we had to flesh the hide and the only place large enough to stretch it out was the back of the cabin. With some effort we lifted the nose to the ridge poles and securely nailed it. After the legs were spread and nailed we measured from the nose to the back pads and the distance was eleven feet 6 inches. We had no salt but were hoping if we kept fleshing all the fat and flesh off the hide it would dry properly. Unfortunately the flies and hot weather got ahead of us and the pelt spoiled.

All was quiet on the bait for a few days so decided to patrol on up the Rocky River to the Rocky Forks cabin. Our plan was to keep a lookout for more bears and instead of travelling the regular trail down Jacques Creek and over the ridge to the Grizzly Cabin we went up Osborne Creek over Osborne Pass and return to the Rocky River where the trail fords the river. There was still snow in the high country and the stream we had to follow down to the main valley once we were across the pass, was in flood. By the time we had come this far we were committed and at every crossing we were nearly washed away. We crossed one at a time and if we lost our footing the one on the bank was there to assist. We made it to the Grizzly cabin and before we could prepare supper we had to try and restore some order to the place which had been totally trashed by bears.

Continuing on up the river the next morning we had to get an early start hoping the melt waters had receded during the night. Our concern was to get across the Rocky River that could be waded under normal conditions.

We made it to the Rocky Forks cabin that afternoon to find it also completely wrecked. No one had been to this cabin for years. Probably the last patrol was made by Dad in the early forties before he was transferred to the Whirlpool District. We had back-packed some supplies with us, enough for a couple of days and then planned to return to Jacques Lake. During the night a heavy downpour started and continued for a couple of days. On our return trip we got to the river crossing, found it in high flood and our only choice was to go back to the cabin and wait.

By now we had used up our food supply and had to resort to salvaging some edibles the bears had left. A small cache of beans was still hanging from the ridge pole which we boiled and flavoured with some crushed horse salt. There was a small amount of flour left in a tin that mice had fouled. An old window screen served as a sieve to separate most solids and from this, mixed with water, made a very flat pancake.

The river continued flooding so the plan was to go downstream about three miles below Stairway Falls and build a raft. We salvaged some telephone wire and found a few spikes which we carried with us. Working our way down to the foot of the falls and looking at the river we decided we would never survive on the kind of raft we could build. We cached the spikes and wire, which I'm sure to this day is still in the rock crevasse where we left them and returned to the cabin.

While waiting around without too much food we checked out some backwater springs below the mouth of the Medicine Tent River looking for fish. The fish were spawning, hard to catch and most unpalatable to eat.

It was about ten days before the river dropped and we could get back to Jacques Lake. Once back at the bait we shot two more grizzlies. With the bait almost gone, we went to work

A dead moose - the results of poor telephone line maintenance.

repairing the telephone line where in a number of instances entangled moose or elk of strangulation.

CHAPTER

4

THE BRAZEAU RIVER DISTRICT

IN early summer fire broke out along the trail near Maligne Pass and threatened to come around the shoulder of Mt. Mary Vaux into the main Maligne Lake valley, which would have for years to come destroyed the natural beauty of this famous valley. My involvement to suppress this fire was to trail 10 pack horses to the mouth of the upper Maligne River and set up a base camp for packing supplies to the fire camp.

Each morning a supply boat would come across Maligne Lake from the end of the road and deliver what had been ordered from the fire boss. My job was to pack everything on to the horses and move it up to the fire camp 12 miles distance. On arrival at the camp I had lots of help unpacking and before I left, all the choice items of food had already been eaten. The return trip to base camp was a race to see who would get there first. In a string of pack horses there is usually a pecking order with the more aggressive horses in the lead and any attempt to change the sequence by a horse not belonging in his subordinate place resulted in fights and races. If two packers worked together some control was possible but alone all you could do was keep up and hope all the gear stayed intact.

The fire burned to timberline and started to come around the shoulder of the mountain when a most welcome rain fell, helping suppress the blaze. Water was at a premium near the fire line and had to be pumped through a series of relay tanks placed at intervals of about 350 feet of vertical rise. The pumps were two cylinder-driven positive pumps and when the back pressure exceeded the power of the motor, it killed the engine.

Once the fire had been subdued, a mop-up crew stood by and my job was to start packing out thousands of feet of dirty wet linen fire hose. Once wet, the hose could not be rolled so had to be folded back and forth in four foot lengths. What had been taken up in panniers of 1000 feet to a pack horse required twice the packing coming out.

From the fire I moved to the Brazeau district and did a reconnaissance of the trails and cabins to determine the extent of deterioration since Warden St. Marie had left to join the army soon after the outbreak of the war. The pack rats had taken over the cabins and travellers had taken liberties with the furnishings and equipment. Most of the phone line over Poboktan Pass was down and the cabins needed re-roofing. I returned to town and got approval to acquire the equipment and materials needed and asked Dad for help to pack it in. The Brazeau cabin was 25 miles in off the highway, Isaac Creek another 18 miles further down the Brazeau River, the Southesk cabin ten miles beyond Isaac Creek on the banks of the Southesk River where the Bighorn trail crosses into the Park and Cairn cabin another ten miles distance at the headwaters of the Cairn River. It took us six weeks to move everything needed at the different cabins and long hours in the evenings repairing and cleaning up. The cabin at Waterfalls, ten miles up from the highway and the Poboktan Pass cabin, built by Warden Don Hoover before the war, were in pretty fair shape and provided satisfactory overnight accommodations when enroute to the Brazeau River area. The eighteen miles from the Brazeau Headquarters to Isaac Creek could be a problem to travel in one day in the winter if snow conditions were poor so Dad and I decided to build a log frame foundation and pole rafter tent frame covered with an 8x10 canvas tent. Two years later Charlie Bowlen and Sam Clifton built the Arete cabin at this site. Another cabin was needed halfway between the Brazeau cabin and Camp Parker via Nigel Pass which was built after the Arete cabin was finished. The location was at the junction of trails from Cline Pass, Jonas Shoulder, Brazeau River and Nigel Pass and called the Four Point cabin.

For years at the Brazeau Headquarters no provision was made for equipment storage except to have it piled inside the cabin. Warden St. Marie must have had plans to change this situation and had cut a set of building logs that was still piled in the yard. Within a few days, Dad and I built a 10'x14' equipment shed and moved the fire suppression equipment out of the cabin. This shelter also provided a proper storage for the saddlery.

In later years, about the mid 80's, I read a newspaper account of the Brazeau Bandit. A drifter had walked into the yard at the Brazeau Headquarters and held Warden Dave Carnell at gun point, ordered him to remove his boots, and locked him in this

(Above) On the left - the original St. Marie shelter. On the right - the cabin builder's camp during the construction of the Arete cabin.
(Below) Brazeau District Headquarters.

very shed. While Dave was held prisoner, the Brazeau Bandit helped himself to some supplies, saddled up the horses and escaped down the river. After Dave broke out of the shed he alerted Headquarters and a ground and air search was unsuccessful in locating the bandit.

After a busy summer, Dad returned to his own district at Athabasca Falls, and I prepared for winter by stocking all the cabins with enough supplies to last until the following June when the passes would be open again for horse travel. October was the time to return to Jasper with the horses and turn them out on their winter range. By now the high country had snow and many of the streams were beginning to freeze over.

The return from the trail head at Pobokton Creek and over the pass to Brazeau Lake had to be by snowshoes. Early winter snowfalls always made for very poor snowshoeing especially in the high country. The snow often hadn't had a chance to settle and laid loose on top of the scrub brush that was common above timberline.

With every step you took your snowshoes would drop through the snow until they settled on the brush and all the loose snow would fall in on top of them. Each step was a major effort and a pace of a mile an hour wasn't uncommon. The thought that often crossed your mind as you looked ahead at the many miles you still had to travel was, "What am I doing here?" It obviously wasn't for the pay of $40.00 a week, so it had to be for the romance of the job. If there is any truth in the belief that you inherit traits from your forefathers, the feeling of wanderlust and adventure came naturally for me.

On my mother's side, my great-grandfather Adolphe Perreault came to Canada from France in 1868 with a Catholic Bishop, Bishop Grandin to work as a carpenter at the St. Albert mission. He married Julie Bernard in 1871 and raised ten children. The second oldest child, Joseph Perreault, my grandfather was born 1875 and in 1893 married my grandmother, Betsy Calder who was the great granddaughter of James Calder who had come to Canada from the Orkney Islands as a Ship's Master for the Hudson Bay Company. Her great grandmother was a native girl, last name Lindsay, believed to be from the York Factory area. Betsy's grandfather and grandmother, Peter Calder and Louise Gadbois's son William married Maria Hamelin and my grandmother was born in 1877 at Slave Lake, Alberta. She died the year my mother was born in 1897 of typhoid.

My father's side of the family tree is more straight forward. My grandfather's parents were Tom and Elizabeth Camp and my grandfather, Thomas Henry was born in 1858 in Derbyshire, England. My grandmother's parents were William and Eliza Perfect and my grandmother was born in 1862 in Long Lane, Bexley, England. My grandparents were married in 1883 and granddad worked with his dad as a wheelwright after serving six years in the Imperial Army. Granddad was the eldest of 21 children, of which 15 lived a long and interesting life, many migrating to Australia and Boston, Mass. USA.

My dad, born 1899, was the youngest of five children. Just prior to migrating to Canada in 1912, Granddad Camp was employed as a greens keeper for a Manor in Bexley Heath, Kent, England. During my navy days, on leave in England I visited my

Grandparents Thomas Henry Camp, 1858-1953, and Maryanne Camp, 1862-1952. Married for 69 years.

dad's birthplace and some of his relatives still living in the same village.

Arriving in Canada, they travelled by train to the end of steel at Wildwood, Alberta and from there with all their possessions on a stone-boat pulled by oxen, settled on a homestead near Anselmo, Alberta. At the age of 18 Dad went to Calgary and joined the Army but the Armistice of November 11, 1918 predated his call-up on his birthday, November 17.

Instead of returning to the homestead he went to Jasper and worked for the Canadian National Railroad as a fireman. It didn't take long before the opportunity to move on came about when he went to work as a trail hand surveying the coal fields up Rock Creek and Grand Cache area. This life style appealed to him and for twenty years travelled extensively through the Rockies from the Peace River to Banff.

My mother, orphaned when only an infant, was taken in by the Grey Nuns and raised at the convent at St. Albert. Her first experience with the outside world was a visit to Jasper when she was nineteen. The mountains terrified her with their closeness and she returned to the convent to work. On her second visit to Jasper a year later she obtained employment as the housemaid for Col. S. Maynard Rogers, the first full time Park Superintendent. The Superintendent's residence was in the building now used as an Information Centre. Her own room was the upper extension on the north side of the building. When the Hotel Red Pass opened in the summer of 1924 she worked there until she married

Dad on November 24th of the same year. The owner of the hotel was Frank Bovin and two years later when I was born, Mom called me after him.

I'm back on the Brazeau intending to stay until Christmas. Jack Christiansen, over on the Rocky River district and I had made plans to meet at Cairn Pass in mid-November and travel back over his district to town. With plenty of time and without the extra work of looking after the horses, I took the opportunity to patrol the many side valleys to get a game count. I also checked some of the old trapper cabins across the Brazeau River and Southesk River to see if there were any recent activities that would indicate I'd have company for the winter.

Poaching right after the war was lucrative with a prime marten pelt bringing over $100. It was always suspected that some of the old time wardens in outlying areas travelled a fine line of honesty. It was easy enough to make a deal with a neighbouring trapper to overlook his activities for a cut of the action. Old marten trap sets were quite often found in the Park, far from where any poacher would dare to travel, but they were there for a reason. Some of the town's highly suspected poachers would casually ask you, when you were in town, how things were going and if you would welcome a visit from them. This was an opening to make some arrangement to overlook their activities in exchange for a bonus. I've often thought, once you committed yourself to this agreement it wouldn't be long before the bonus was cut off and the poaching increased, knowing your job would be on the line if you tried to stop.

Trapper's cabin - Brazeau River, at Latitude 52 degrees, 25 Minutes.

The Alberta Forest Service had a cabin a mile north of the Southesk cabin they seldom used but was a popular campsite for hunters and provided easy access over the unmarked Park boundary to some excellent sheep range. A trapper's cabin between the Forestry cabin and the boundary was also worth checking out occasionally. When making a foot patrol before the Southesk River froze over, the forestry bridge at the river crossing was used when travelling to the Cairn cabin.

As it happened when on my way to the Cairn cabin to meet Jack Christiansen I picked up an old snowshoe trail at the forks of the Cairn and Southesk rivers in the Southesk valley. I stopped to boil the tea pail to make up my mind to either continue up the Southesk following a rather old, questionable snowshoe trail I still could not decide which direction the traveller was going, or go up to the Cairn cabin. The decision was to go to the Cairn cabin. The next day I rendezvoused with Jack in the Pass. At the cabin that night we discussed my concern

Original Forest Service bridge crossing Southesk River on Big Horn Trail.

about the possibility of someone with a winter camp at Southesk Lake and decided to go and have a look. The lake was about twenty miles distance. We were not equipped for an extended winter campout but with a bedroll and enough food pre-cooked, left the next morning. As is common with most people travelling in the mountains, when getting together in town you exchange information about access trails to various places to which you've been or intend to go. I recalled someone telling me you could take a short-cut over the shoulder of Southesk Mountain from the Cairn river and cut off a few miles from the regular trail. This is what we decided to do but soon regretted our decision.

The climb was steep and by the time we had reached the summit the snow was deep and heavy. Descending into the Southesk valley wasn't much easier as the snowshoes would slide ahead and bury themselves until you stopped and pulled them back to the surface. By late afternoon we had reached Southesk lake and concluded that if a poacher was working this area he would camp across the lake with the advantage if someone approached he would see them long before they arrived at his site. A winter crossing of any lake in the mountains at higher elevations can be extremely dangerous.

When heavy snow falls before the lake freezes over it creates a condition that clear ice does not form under the snow. As more snow falls the weight of the new snow forces water to flood over the old ice. You can be way out on the lake before this becomes apparent. As you look back at the water on your snowshoe trail and at the same time with your snowshoes collecting slush ice, your only option is to keep moving towards the closest shore.

Tired and cautious we skirted the lake staying close to shore and had no trouble. At no time during the day did we cut any fresh tracks to indicate recent activity in the valley. Reaching the timber at the head of the lake, we built a pole leanto and a big fire with a reflector out of a green log.

It was a cold night and before dawn we had agreed we weren't going to accomplish very much hanging around this valley. In the dark we packed up our meagre outfit, put on our snowshoes and headed back down the valley. It was still too dark to see far but we decided our chances of going directly across the lake were good. It may not have been the smartest thing to do but we made it safely across.

Once it was daylight we could follow our trail from yesterday and when we reached the point where we had descended the mountain we decided against returning that way. It meant breaking trail but we soon reached the forks of the rivers and my tracks of three days before.

It's a steady climb back up the Cairn River to the cabin and it was dark once more before we arrived. The thermometer registered minus 22 degrees F. but soon the cabin was warm and we turned in without supper. The round trip had been over 40 miles so the next day was needed to recuperate. The return trip to Jasper via the Rocky River was without incident and was timed to be home for Christmas.

CHAPTER

THE HAZARDS OF TRAVELLING ALONE

R ETURNING to the Brazeau District after the holidays I decided to use skis instead of snowshoes. Starting from the trail head at Poboktan cabin I put climbing skins on my skis and started up the trail towards the Waterfalls cabin en route to Poboktan Pass.

Skiing was becoming a popular winter sport and there were many opinions pro and con about skis versus snowshoes for winter travel. To begin with, the need for special footwear, skis, poles, wax and climbing skins all added to the basic equipment you still needed for winter travel as compared to a pair of snowshoes. Once arrived at a campsite or cabin, skis are difficult to manage going to the outhouse, fetching water or cutting wood. For the pro-ski people the obvious solution was a pair of snowshoes at each cabin although this didn't solve the problem of winter campsites.

I thought this trip would be an opportunity for me to make a first-hand assessment of the controversy. I started up the trail and stopped at Poligne Creek for lunch. Soon a fire was going and the teapail boiling. Lunch was a selection of Christmas goodies, especially Christmas cake, a source of high energy.

After lunch I had terrible pains in my stomach. I doubled up with cramps and tried to think of what I could do to stop the pain. In my pack I carried a bottle of Absorbine Liniment and baring my stomach to the fire gave myself a good rubdown. The heat of the fire combined with the heat of the liniment soon started a slow burn on my stomach that overshadowed the internal pain.

I had no intention of spending the night beside a campfire so packed up and continued on to the Waterfalls cabin. By now the liniment burn had subsided and the internal pain returned more severely. After starting the fire I phoned the Warden's switch-board and asked if they could patch me through to Dr. O'Hagan's office. I spoke to the doctor and his diagnosis was a possible appendix attack and told me to put a cold compress on the location of the pain, have some rest and call again in the morning. I spent a very uncomfortable night and after talking to the doctor again, decided I'd better return to town.

The downhill trail to the highway was no advantage for skis as I was out of control most of the time and preoccupied with the pain. I couldn't help thinking of Frank Burstrom when years ago he had a similar experience over at Brazeau Lake. With a severe appendix attack he strapped an ice pack to his stomach and snowshoed from the lake over Poboktan Pass and down to the highway. Arriving at the highway, which hadn't been ploughed, he continued down the road until he met his rescuers.

When I reached the highway, a vehicle was waiting and I went into town and to the doctor's office. In the Doctor's opinion, my condition was not critical and he recommended I go to the Colonel Mewburn Veteran Hospital in Edmonton, as I still qualified for veterans' benefits, saving the personal cost of the operation. I caught the next train to Edmonton and was soon on the operating table. Memories of that cold, brightly lit, stainless steel and stark white enamel operating room are easy to recall especially in comparison to the one-room cabin I had left just two days before.

The recovery room was the public ward where 27 other beds were occupied by veterans suffering from untold injuries that didn't inhibit their sense of humour. The four nurses on duty all the time were very capable of handling the sick but very funny jokes and comments. The effort to keep from laughing to avoid the consequences of severe pain from my recent incision was almost impossible.

After a couple of weeks I was discharged and spent a few days in the city before returning to Jasper and back to the district on snowshoes this time, having decided snowshoe travel was more appropriate for backcountry winter travel.

By mid-February the snow pack in the high country settles and the days are longer. I was glad to be back on my district and make snowshoe patrols into the side valleys under ideal conditions. It was an opportunity to observe and count wildlife still on their winter range. The winter of 1947-48 was a year of heavy snowfall and the elk mortality was high. Along the Brazeau River from the Dowling ford to Brazeau Lake it averaged one dead elk a mile was observed from the trail. To extrapolate from this observation an estimate could be misleading. It was expected that

Southesk Lake area game count with Canadian Wildlife Biologist, Dean Fisher.

many died but the elk slaughter continued in the Athabasca valley.

In the same period of time the sheep population in Cairn Pass had drastically declined. In the late 1930's Dr. Ian McTaggart-Cowan, a Canadian Wildlife Service biologist, reported large numbers of sheep in the general area of Cairn Pass that had now dwindled to a few scattered bands in the same area. Dr. Dean Fisher, also a C.W.S. biologist spent a month with me trying to determine if my present observations were incomplete or in fact there were less sheep. The conclusion was less sheep but with no obvious reason.

To be certain the sheep had not moved to another range we went back from Cairn cabin to the Southesk River and up the Southesk to Southesk Lake and camped.

Just downriver from Southesk Lake along the riverbank on our way up to the lake we were taken by surprise by a string of pack horses travelling full out. By the time I'd collected myself some riders came into view and I asked them to pull up for a moment. The spokesman for the group was a woman and when she stopped to talk the rest of the party moved on. Her name was Myrtle, a sister of the Sans brothers that outfitted out of Nordegg. From previous experience I had some concern about her presence in the Park but I was outmanouvered and she rode off to catch up with her party. To this day I've regretted not being more assertive, stopping the whole outfit and have them unpack. If not a trophy I would have expected to find an excessive load of fish as the lake was an exceptional lake for Dolly Varden. I'll never know.

My campsite in the Restless River basin.

The next day we went over Southesk Pass and were impressed by the distance from timberline to timberline which is about 9 miles. The view of the east face of Maligne Mountain is spectacular and can only be seen from Southesk Pass. It is one huge glacier from summit to base and the view far surpasses that seen from Maligne Lake. Once we reached the Rocky River an old fire burn makes it impossible to follow the trail. Windfall was everywhere until we reached the valley floor. I intended to camp at the mouth of Helmet Creek at an old campsite called the Butterbox but it looked like a poor place to hold horses.

On one of my previous patrols out from the Rocky Forks cabin I had scouted the Restless River watershed and located a game trail leading in to a huge basin with good horse feed so we pushed on. We set up a camp in the basin and spent a couple of days looking for sheep. The Restless River valley reaches almost to a high summit which could be crossed coming out above Southesk Lake. The only game we saw in the valley was a couple of goats.

Wolves were on the increase and although not proven conclusively were considered a contributing factor in the decline of the sheep. This observation in part helped support the Parks attitude toward wolves as an undesirable park resident.

All wardens were encouraged to shoot, snare or poison all the wolves they could. Coyotes also came under this classification and often a warden's ability and effectiveness was measured by the number of pelts he brought to town each month. Warden Frank Burstrom was usually number one having the Devona District. Excellent winter range for game with open hillsides and grasslands gave him the advantage. Warden Frank Bryant had Russian Wolf hounds that could run down and kill coyotes on frozen lakes. Warden Frank Wells kept cougar hounds to tree cougars. The success of the cougar hunt was demonstrated by bringing the dead animal to show the school kids and hanging the pelts on the corral fence. On the Brazeau I was having some success with wolf snares. Frankly speaking the predators didn't have much chance of survival.

Of note, in the August 1953 Journal of Mammalogy is an item by Dr. Banfield. Very little information was known about the range of the individual wolf but two wolf pups tagged and recaptured gave some additional information. One pup tagged July 3, 1946 on the Panther River in Banff was taken by a trapper, Clarence Long, near the Ya-ha-Tinda ranch on April 11, 1950 only 16 miles from the den site. On June 13th 1949, Warden Ernie Stenton tagged a wolf pup on the Cascade River in Banff and on November 12th 1951 I snared this wolf, now fully grown, near Isaac Creek. To reach this point the wolf had had to cross seven major river valleys with the shortest distance between the tagging and capture of 162 miles.

As time went by the wardens became more sophisticated and efficient in their efforts to eliminate predators. Cyanide guns were obtained that worked on a trigger device that had a firing pin and a cartridge loaded with cyanide about the same size as a .38 revolver shell casing. Bait was attached to the cylinder and nailed to a tree about 18" above ground. When any animal of the size and strength to bite the bait and pull the trigger firing the device, the poison entered the throat and death was instant. Then 1080 was introduced. This was extremely lethal and required training to use. It came in liquid form and had to be injected into a freshly shot bait. One drop into your eye was enough to kill you. Again is was unselective, killing small fur-bearing animals, eagles, ravens and anything else that fed on the bait. It had one advantage over strychnine. Being water soluble it leached into the ground in the spring, whereas strychnine if not recovered continues to kill in the subsequent food chain.

Warden Jack Christiansen who had transferred to the Smoky River district was doing his share to kill predators. He had a habit of partially smoking a cigarette and putting the butt in his shirt pocket to be smoked later. He also kept refills for his cyanide guns in the same shirt pocket. Nearing his patrol cabin one evening he lit up a butt and approached the yard when he began to feel very unsteady, had difficulty reaching the door and going inside. He concluded that somehow he had poisoned himself and his first thought was to leave a message to whomever came and found his body.

Reaching for a calendar on the wall he pulled it to the table and turned it over and wrote what he considered a clear and concise message. He blacked out and later that evening he woke in total darkness, nearly frozen but still alive. After lighting the lantern and starting a fire he remembered the message he had written on the back of the calendar. To his utter astonishment what he saw was a scrawl of pencil marks that had no resemblance to a written message. When he related this story to me what had impressed him the most was how clearly he thought he had written.

With the help of old pictures to remind me of events, I remember that I went back to the Rocky River district in the spring of 1948. Jack was now on the Smoky River and a new man had been hired. Louis Reese was his name, a veteran from the Air Force. He may be best remembered by the townspeople of his ability in a barroom to recite old English prose such as ballads of the Crusaders. On his discharge from the service his adjustment to civilian life was difficult, and with the help of his brother, decided to be a trapper. He bought a trapline at Fortress Lake from Charlie Blackman of Tete Jaune Cache. He hoped the outdoors, a challenging job and distance from temptation would help him settle down.

His main cabin was at the east end of Fortress Lake with access from Sunwapta Falls, across the Athabasca River and up the Chaba River, a distance of about twelve miles. After getting established and setting a few traps around the lake he decided to go to the far end of the lake to another cabin he had been told was there to work the headwaters of the Wood River. Arriving late in the afternoon he found the cabin but heavy snows had collapsed the roof. The ridge pole had broken in the centre and when the roof caved in it had left the inside corners of the cabin protected from the snow. With only a sleeping bag and a few supplies he decided to build an open fire in one of the corners and try to keep warm until daylight before returning to his main cabin. The fire burned poorly and the wet logs gave off a steamy strong smoke that bothered him. Sitting in the dark and not knowing what was happening and waiting for daylight, he finally realized the irritation in his eyes from the smoke had all but completely blinded him.

Crawling outside he panicked when all he could make out was the faint outline between the sky and the treetops. Knowing he could not travel he had to go back into his shelter and wait to see what would happen to his eyes. After the second night he couldn't stand it any longer and decided in order to survive he had to return to the main cabin. Once out on the lake he was fortunate enough that the lake was narrow and long and he could make out his direction of travel. Reaching the cabin he stayed close by until his eyesight improved sufficiently to travel back to the highway and town. Charlie Blackman took the trapline back and Louis joined the Warden Service. Unfamiliar with the country and no experience with horses, my job was to make an orientation trip with Louis to the Rocky River.

CHAPTER

6

MAINTENANCE – TRAILS – CABINS – COMMUNICATIONS & EQUIPMENT

BACK on the Brazeau for the summer my first task was to repair the telephone line over Poboktan Pass and replace many of the old poles that had fallen. Communication with the Jasper Headquarters had always been poor with no regular schedule to check on your activities or safety. Most of the time it was assumed the line was down but it was a comfort to know if you had an emergency you could call for help.

One job I had promised myself to complete this summer was to dig a root cellar beneath the cabin floor so next winter I could keep perishables without freezing. After removing the heater from the centre of the room and lifting a section of the floor, I began excavating. The digging was hard as the soil was made up of riverbed gravel. The first step was to shovel the earth on to the cabin floor, the second step to throw it out the window, and the third step remove it from the side of the cabin. As I dug deeper the sides of the hole continually caved in, and the deeper I went down the wider the hole became until I started shoring with logs and backfilling behind the logs. I finally ended up with a 5'x5' cellar 5' deep.

Park Warden Louis Reese looking over his district.

As a labour-saving plan to haul the gravel from the yard I removed the steel tub from a wheelbarrow and secured a ring to the front. The idea was that once I loaded it with gravel I would hook up the old skid horse, Blue, to this conveyance and have him pull it over to the river bank where it would automatically dump. Blue had been used to skid the new telephone poles over Poboktan Pass and was well broke and gentle but this was a new experience for him. My first mistake was to load the tub too heavy and secondly, take it for granted all would go well. As soon as Blue got the load moving it ran over some rocks and the noise it made of steel scratching over rock sent shivers down our backs. That was enough to set Blue into complete uncontrollable panic. As soon as the gravel had bounced out of the tub all I could see was Blue kicking at the tub that kept landing on his back, falling off and getting kicked again, all in sequence to a full gallop across the flats and into the timber on the far side of the clearing.

When I finally caught up to him all tangled up in the wind-fallen timber, he had been subdued to a wild-eyed, shaking, sweating, terrified animal. Even after I had taken the skid harness off and released him he stood for the longest time motionless, afraid to move in case that horrible noise started again. I returned to the more conventional method of removing the gravel by reassembling the wheelbarrow and hauling it myself.

Another long-planned but never initiated job I was determined to start this summer was to build a secure drift fence to keep my horses closer to the cabin. Last year I had some of the horses that had been brought over from Sundre and all they had on their minds was to go back home. One morning after working them the previous day and turning them loose with hobbles to graze, I went to bring them in before having my breakfast. After hanging around near the cabin for a while where the grass was good they wandered off down the river. Usually in the evening you take a walk to see how the horses are doing but I went fishing instead without too much concern as to their whereabouts.

I soon picked up their tracks and the farther the distance travelled, the straighter their tracks became, until four hours later and twelve miles from the cabin, I caught them on Job Creek flats as they were getting ready to cross the Brazeau River and start up the Job Creek trail or down the far side of the river. A short time later with the horses on one side of the river and me on the other side, my problems would have been greater. I caught the best saddle horse and bridled her before taking the hobbles off the rest of the horses. Then, jumping on bareback I started hazing them back to the cabin. Everything was going well until they started fighting for the lead and trying to pass one another until it turned into a race to see who could reach the cabin first. Riding bareback at the best of times isn't the most comfortable way to travel but riding at a gallop on a horse wet with sweat, it wasn't long before I started losing skin off my tail-bone. The trip back was made in record time and I soon had them all tied up where I intended to keep them for the night.

That evening Jeff Wilson pulled in with a group of trail riders and after supper I went and sat beside their campfire to visit. Relating to Jeff my day's experience, his advice was "hobble their back feet". So that night, that's what I did but it wasn't long before they were out of sight again. Next morning I was up and away and within a mile found some very quiet horses standing in a meadow. After their first burst of energy to leave, the hobbles had almost crippled their back legs. They had spent the night with their hind feet in one spot and had side-stepped in a circular motion with their front feet while they fed. I was concerned that if they stood nearly motionless their muscles would stiffen up and they would be unable to travel. I had planned to go over Nigel Pass to the highway that day so packed up and left. The walking and letting them stand in the cold water at every river crossing relieved the soreness and we finished the trip with no long-term effects.

All these problems were fresh in my mind and the building of the drift fence started. As a general rule for meals, what I cooked for supper, the leftovers were warmed for breakfast. This one morning I had a two day leftover mulligan to eat, and afterwards left for the drift fence site two miles down the river. Soon after starting work I broke out in a cold sweat and began having double vision so I returned back up the trail to the cabin. Still seeing double I stumbled along sick to my stomach. I remember reaching the cabin and passed out on the bed.

Sometime during the night I woke up, cold and confused, lit the fire, had some tea and went to bed. That was the end of my casual cooking routine. I suspected food poisoning and from then on became more careful. I did finish the fence and no longer worried about losing my horses.

This was the year for the builders to build log cabins at Arete and Four Point so again I asked for help to pack in materials and supplies. Dad volunteered to do the packing and with the two of us and six pack horses we soon had everything in place.

Lumber cut into four foot lengths and 18 pieces to a bundle made a side pack. With two side packs to a horse it took 10 pack-horse loads to cover the roof and floor of each cabin. With the other supplies needed, it took three weeks to get everything on

(Above left) Arete Shelter, 1948 – built by Charlie Bowlen and Sam Clifton.
(Above right) An exceptionally large buffalo skull.

site at the Arete shelter and only a couple of weeks more for Four Point by packing over Nigel Pass. By fall the cabins were complete with a few good weeks of weather left to patrol to the far end of the district, which had been neglected all summer.

Dr. Don Flook, another Canadian Wildlife Service Biologist, made a late fall patrol with me to reassess the game population and set up some range plots on Chocolate Mountain to establish the forage impact the sheep had on winter range. Of special interest, we were also looking for an old buffalo skull I'd previously found and taken pictures of, near the Southesk cabin. The skull was of unusually large size with the core of the horns over 30" from tip to tip. With a little imagination, by adding the horns over the tips of the core, the head of this buffalo must have been enormous. We were disappointed not finding it but I'm thankful I have it recorded in a picture.

Fred Brewster, an early day Guide and Outfitter from Jasper, reported finding the remains of a buffalo carcass along the shore of Brazeau Lake in the early thirties that still had some hair and hide attached. It's fascinating to think of how some old bull buffalo were pushed back into the mountains by hunting pressure and lived out their solitary lives for years without being detected. The last recorded sighting of buffalo that I know of was when Franchere travelled through Buffalo Prairie in the Athabasca valley in 1814.

The Brazeau district covered an area of about 550 square miles. One section I had yet to investigate was the Don Hoover trail from Isaac cabin over the southwest shoulder of Mt. Dalhousie and down a tributary of the Southesk River to a point on the river midway between the Southesk cabin and Southesk Lake. It was sometimes referred to as the Indian Cut-off trail and Don

Hoover had used it occasionally.

The trail was poorly marked but eventually we were out of the timber and crossing a high summit over 8000 feet. The view was spectacular. Don Flook and I sat for some time in the warm fall sun, glassing the mountainsides without seeing any sign of game. Descending on the Southesk watershed we stopped for lunch in a meadow and let the horses feed.

When on the trail, lunch was nearly always a can of sardines which it was that day. When I finished I cast the empty can aside and to this day remember clearly Don's admonition of what I had done. In his very tactful way he explained how litter, especially in the high country, distracts from the natural beauty of the surroundings and would be here for years if left. For a moment I thought he was kidding but the serious tone of his voice convinced me he meant what he said. From that day on I kept my own pack-in, pack-out policy not to litter.

After a few more days of beautiful fall weather the mountains had a dusting of snow on the peaks and ice was starting to form on the creeks so it was time to move back to the main valley and make one last trip with the horses to pack in my winter supplies.

The winter of 1948-49 was nothing special. The first trip over the pass on snowshoes was difficult but once in the Brazeau River valley the conditions were pleasant. The first task was to get some fresh meat and I hunted until I shot a young bull elk.

A standard item at most cabins was a meat cache. Built on a platform high between two trees with the tops cut off and with stove pipe around the bottoms, it kept animals from climbing to the meat. Once properly butchered, the meat placed in a cache would cure and freeze lasting all winter. A good axe was all that was required to chop off some stew meat. The fishing was good and always a change from a meat diet.

A patrol to the Cairn cabin was planned and the most memorable event of the whole trip happened during the night. I had stopped at Arete cabin, had supper and gone to bed. For some reason I woke up and couldn't believe my eyes.

The northern lights were putting on a display far beyond anything I had ever witnessed. The entire valley and mountains were constantly being lit up in brilliant colours of red, blue, green and oranges, in more of sheets of light than of rays of light usually associated with the Northern lights. It was spell-binding and for a long time I stood watching and wondering if I was seeing the world come to an end. I was thankful when the lights went out and darkness came once more. I felt so privileged to having had the experience of such a natural phenomenon. My only regret was that I couldn't share it with someone.

DIVERSIONS FROM THE ISOLATED LIFESTYLE OF A DISTRICT WARDEN THE ELK SLAUGHTER AND OTHER ASSIGNMENTS

B Y the middle of December I had worked my way back to the Brazeau Headquarters and on to town for Christmas. I put in some time on the elk hunt after the holidays, which was a welcome assignment as opposed to returning to the District.

The elk herd reduction program, as it was formally called, was a very basic unsophisticated operation that had as it's primary purpose reduction of the elk population. Over the years there was very little change in the method of operation.

Two wardens who had been on this exercise from the beginning were George Camp and George Fowlie, referred to by the rest of the crew as "the Georges". They ran the show and provided the continuity needed for the rest of the hunters who came and went depending on who was available.

Each morning of the hunt before daylight the convoy of hunters and vehicles travelled to an area of the park where it was expected the elk may be grazing. After a herd of elk was located a general plan was discussed and agreed upon, more to keep everyone aware what the rest were doing in order not to be shot when the firing started.

Catching the herd in a crossfire produced the best results but hard on the nerves when stray bullets were ricocheting around where you were crouched down. Whatever you shot you bled and gutted, regrouped to take an inventory of the number downed and their location. The next part of the operation was to skid them with a four wheel drive vehicle to a common yarding area where everyone assisted in skinning the hides off and loading the carcasses on to a truck. A good day's hunt produced about 20 animals.

In town the carcasses were split down the back and with meat hooks hung on the rafters of the hay shed. When the shed was full, about 100 carcasses, they were quartered and shipped by railroad freight to the designated Indian reserves. The hides went to the mission schools for tanning to be made into moccasins and mitts. The antlers were sent to a cutlery factory to be used for stag-horn knife handles.

The work was hard, especially in sub-zero weather. Skinning with bare hands, removing the hide on the frozen legs and belly often resulted in cuts, self-inflicted or from someone else. Infection was always a concern and we carried a disinfectant for immediate first-aid.

You could easily fall into disfavour with your fellow workers if you did one of two things. Firstly, wound an elk and follow it into the back country that was inaccessible by vehicle, kill the animal and then walk out and ask for help to skid it by hand back to the road. Secondly, at just about quitting time come across a herd when by yourself, and drop four or five animals that had to be gutted and skinned before going home and then working on into the evening to get them split and hung.

I pulled this stunt only once when a herd crossed my trail when I was coming back to the truck empty handed late in the afternoon. In a matter of a few minutes I had eight elk laid out on the flats close to the railroad station of Henry House. My skill as a hunter was rewarded by the deafening silence of tired men as we worked on into the night.

That winter another new warden was hired, Tom Ross, a Navy veteran. When he arrived home he went to work for Red Creighton as a trail hand and cook for hunting parties. He had spent the winters as a trapper with Red and Art Allen on the Jackpine River, a tributary of the Smoky River before deciding to become a Park Warden. Tom's qualifications to be a warden were excellent having lived in Jasper most of his life, he knew the country and the people. His interest was in the outdoors and had all the ability of a back-country traveller.

I was pleased when Chief Warden Charlie Phillips suggested that Tom accompany me on a snowshoe patrol of the Brazeau District. We left Jasper in late January and for a month covered the district as far as the Cairn cabin and returned. We both considered ourselves experts on snowshoes and each day there was silent competition in our ability to travel fast, maybe leave the other behind or ask the one in front to step aside as it appeared he was getting tired. We also kept a record of travel time between the patrol cabins and on the return trip tried to better our own time. There was a disadvantage in this routine because we never

Tom Ross – a new recruit to the Park Warden Service at the stop-over shelter near the Jonas cut-off trail junction.

took the time to look the country over.

On lay-over days we made up for it by side-trip patrols and making game observations. In contemplation of these early days there was a great deal of information about the Park recorded by wardens on back country patrols. However, this information had no way of eventually going into a system for permanent safe keeping and retrieval. Only memories and personal journals are left, and memories especially are fast fading away. The most common inaccurate general statement that can be made is, "It's not as good as it was in the old days." In many instances I'm sure it's better.

The spring of '49 found me back once more on the Rocky River district on another orientation trip with another new warden. Louis Reese faded into obscurity and Bert Longson and his lady friend, Ann, moved on to the district. Bert was an army veteran and had spent some time in the bush out from Beaverlodge in northwestern Alberta.

In the short time I was with Bert and Ann, I had the feeling that Bert thought I'd been assigned to him as his assistant. Our days started when I got up in the morning to start the fire and go look for the horses. After a casual breakfast I saddled up and made preparations to travel. On the trail, Bert rode lead and I looked after the outfit. It was on one of these days when we were returning to Jacques Lake that four grizzlies stood on the trail ahead of us.

The river was on one side of the trail and a steep cutbank from on old river bed on the other side. The bears were as startled as we were as the noise of the river had drowned out the sound of our approach. As soon as they saw us they took flight up the cutbank having difficulty getting their footing in the loose gravel.

Bert's reaction was to unsheathe his rifle from the scabbard and as the last grizzly crested the top of the bank, he shot it. Down it came, right into the middle of the pack outfit and for reasons unknown had only one thing on his mind. He looked like a two year old who wanted to catch up to his mother so back up the bank he went and over the top. Bert's firepower was a .300 lever action Savage that at one time belonged to Warden Alex Nellis. It had been a good saddle gun but was worn out from years of use.

The last time I remember running into a similar situation was with Dad in 1940 as we approached the crossing on the Medicine Tent near Rocky Forks. We were in the burnt-over section of the trail with small pockets of green timber that had not been touched by the fire.

Coming down the trail to meet us were four grizzlies travelling in single file and unaware of our presence. Dad hollered out to them which got their attention but didn't seem to change their plan. We both dismounted and as Dad pulled his rifle from the scabbard, suggested to me to get up a tree. He cocked his rifle and turned to me to ask where I was. In that short period of time I was up a lodgepole pine about 30 feet and Dad dusted the trail with his .270 Winchester in front of the lead bear. They took the hint, left the trail and circled around us continuing on their way downriver.

The next morning, on this same trip, stands out clearly in my mind. It was common practise to pile your saddlery on the cabin porch for safe keeping and give the saddle blankets a chance to dry. There was only one problem with this—the porcupines and deer liked to come to eat or lick the leather for the salt from the horse sweat. Usually the first thing to go were the ladigos (cinch straps).

Just after daylight a noise on the porch had awakened us and Dad, grumbling to himself about the dammed deer, went to the cabin door in his long johns, opened it and taking a step outside let out a holler. To his total surprise, a large black bear standing on his hind legs woofed right back at him face to face. The door was slammed quickly in the bear's face.

Another incident that happened in 1946 at the Cairn cabin

when Dad was helping me get established on the Brazeau district had a similar storyline except for one difference. Again a bear was on the porch and Dad had gone to investigate. I was lying on my bunk after lunch at the time facing the door and saw the bear to one side of where Dad was standing. My rifle was above my bed so I reached for it and shot the bear while sitting up in my bunk. The crack of the rifle in the cabin, and the bear dropping at my Dad's feet wasn't Dad's idea of a joke although the look on his face left me doubled up laughing. Once he recovered I was given a stern warning about shooting accidents. Soon all was forgotten and we skinned the bear, cutting off the most choice cuts which we ate.

....Once Bert and Ann were settled I left for the Brazeau. Soon after, I started to be unsettled with my lifestyle. Based on the fact that I had the ability to handle horses, and snowshoes and look after myself in the back-country, there was every indication I would be continually passed up when a highway district became vacant. Staying on the Brazeau forever wasn't my idea of a career. The response I received from the Chief Warden when confronted with my concern was that he had to keep the less qualified new wardens closer to town to help them out and keep an eye on them. Besides that, they had families that needed them and it wasn't safe for them to go in to the back country alone.

This was some consolation to me and satisfied my ego for the time being. I was having a good summer except my energy level was so high I couldn't sit still and relax.

I climbed to the top of mountains, looking for lakes I had only seen on a map, scouting out old trails and Indian campsites and anything else to keep me occupied. The more energy I expended the less I slept and the poorer I ate. On a month-end trip into town I visited Dr. O'Hagan who had been our family doctor to see if he could help me settle down.

His opinion was I suffered from a vitamin deficiency and prescribed some medicine. On the return trip back to the district I asked my mother to come along and maybe some good home-cooked meals would help. She was also an avid fisherman and with the glowing stories of how great the fishing was, she didn't need any more encouragement.

I had built a rather elaborate raft with oars at Brazeau Lake, a mile from the cabin, to get out to where the big fish were but the glacial silt in the water made for poor fishing. There were always pan-size fish to catch in the river behind the cabin so all was not lost.

After Mom returned to her home at Athabasca Falls, I started feeling restless again and fell back into my old routine, so paid

Louise Camp at Brazeau Headquarters, 1949.

Dr. O'Hagen another visit. This time he made the observation I was getting "bushed" which to me sounded like I was going a little crazy. What I didn't realize was my nerves were wired so tight that I couldn't relax and enjoy myself. Dr. O'Hagen advised it was time to get out of the bush for awhile.

I took this information to the Chief Warden and with a veil of threat stated if I couldn't transfer to a highway district I'd quit. I guess no manager likes to be given an ultimatum and he suggested I quit. I finished off the summer and in the fall with the help of two friends, Len Gaddy and Dale Mainprize, went over the district and packed out all my personal possessions and supplies.

CHAPTER

8

BACK TO CIVILIZATION
BUT STILL IN TOUCH WITH THE
PARK WARDEN SERVICE

WITH what little savings I had I took off on a holiday to Vancouver and Seattle returning home broke. Going back to the Chief Warden, I asked if he would give me a job. The Warden Service had their own maintenance staff and programs that included cabin building, trail and bridge construction and a sawmill up the Whirlpool River. I accepted a position as a labourer at the sawmill and enjoyed the experience working at a variety of jobs.

It was a small crew but we had a cookshack and bunkhouse. In early spring the garbage, that over the winter had accumulated in a frozen pile outside the bunkhouse, was a great attraction for the bears just out of hibernation. All night long they would rummage through the pile of half frozen waste and when not eating they were fighting. Some of the crew were really bothered, not being able to sleep because of the racket.

Packing out from Isaac Creek cabin. Mounted are wardens Ed Brennen and Norm Hooper, myself and Len Gaddy standing.

Climbing into Poboktan Pass from the Brazeau valley are Len Gaddy and Dale Mainprize.

Although the bears were protected an ingenious device was developed to scare them away. A couple of sticks of dynamite, with a detonator and electric wire running back to a plunger in the bunkhouse, was buried in the garbage pile. At the opportune time when bears gathered over the charge, it was detonated, blowing garbage into the air and sending the bears scattering in all directions. It wasn't very effective and soon the bears wandered back and the cycle started all over again. The greatest reaction was from some members of the crew who were not aware of when the dynamite was to be set off, especially those who were asleep.

A story told to me by Bruce Otto, when I worked with him in 1942 on the trail to the Tonquin valley was similar to this one but with a different twist. At Bruce's tie-hacking camp, bears were also fighting in the garbage dump keeping the men awake. This camp was located a mile beyond the first tie-camp. The buildings were made of rough-sawn lumber and covered with tar paper. Unknown to the men, Bruce had obtained a wooden barrel in which he placed about 6 sticks of dynamite and around the charge, filled with rocks about the size of golf balls. The ignition device was a crossarm nailed above the barrel, with a fish head at one end and a nail driven through the crossarm directly in line with the detonator secured in the dynamite. The principle behind this device was when a bear pulled on the fish head the crossarm pivoted with the nail coming down on the detonator and setting off the charge.

Bruce went out in the evening and set up his time bomb and

(Above) Bill Cleveland's telephone crew. With Bill and Kevin, Slim and Mrs. Fry and Cam Taylor.
(Right) Geraldine Lookout tower under construction, 1950.

went back to the bunkhouse to wait. It was sometime during the night when one of the many bears pulled the trigger and the bomb exploded. It even took Bruce by surprise when he heard and saw the results. Not only the wounded but not-so wounded bears took off in all directions. Most of the men, hearing this terrible noise of rocks falling on the bunkhouse, evacuated the camp immediately. When Bruce looked out all he could see were bears and men in their long-johns running flat out side by side away from the camp.

In the spring I transferred to Bill Cleveland's telephone line crew that was building a line to the Geraldine Lookout tower site. With the line construction completed I moved up to the tower site to help construct the 50 foot steel fire lookout tower. Harvey Crate was in charge of this project. Harvey had been in the Warden Service at the beginning of the war and went overseas as a dispatch rider for the Army. One day while on dispatch in England he hit a rock fence and was badly injured. When he regained consciousness he had a complete loss of memory. He spent many months convalescing and was finally sent home in the care of a special nurse who was to help him adjust to a life he couldn't remember. He had some recall when he heard his Dad's voice which helped him remember his past. One of his jobs was to build a new log cabin at Jacques Lake. He was an expert axman and before he went overseas had helped his dad and brother build a chalet at Lucerne Lake. His friends and associates had the idea if he returned to some familiar work, his recovery would be faster.

The first phase of the Jacques Lake project was to build a 10'x12' equipment shed on a cement foundation. Harvey worked with meticulous care and the shed was a masterpiece. His one problem was he wanted to do everything himself without assistance from the rest of the crew and the job took forever. The Chief Warden's reaction to this dilemma was, "Forget the craftsmanship and erect the main building as quickly as possible and go on to another job." The results were, the cabin was poorly constructed and Warden Clarence Wilkins spent the following winter trying to improve the interior. When I took over the district on April 9, 1952 I continued the work and added partitions and furniture.

With the fire tower at Geraldine Lookout completed I worked with the trail crew on the Devona Fire Road. We camped on the side of the road just beyond Windy Point and when the work of upgrading the road was complete I quit.

A friend of mine, Earl Ketchison was getting married in Winnipeg, and I had plans to drive with Jim Donnelly to the wedding. Earl had arrived in Jasper after the war following his imprisonment in a prisoner-of-war camp in Europe. He worked on the railroad and then became a food and drug inspector in Winnipeg, checking food contamination resulting from floodwaters. He transferred to Vancouver and worked in the Dockyards checking shipments of food arriving from overseas. On our return from Winnipeg we stopped in Edmonton to visit with Jim's brother, Francis. The previous winter, Jasper held a winter carnival and the carnival queen was Lucille Dubord from Edmonton. Francis had a great attraction towards Lucille and decided to transfer his position with the C.N. Railroad from Jasper to Edmonton.

It was expected that Francis would arrange a party with a few of Lucille's friends when we arrived in Edmonton. Lucille had a sister, Edna, which Francis paired up with Jim and my date was another attractive girl name Tillie de Rappard. We had a good

Moving Curly Phillip's boat building shed to Ed Neighbor's site on Pyramid Road.

time with one exception. To me, Edna should have been my date. Within a few days I discreetly arranged to have it my way and for the time we spent in Edmonton, Edna was my date.

By now, with all our travelling and trying to impress the girls in Edmonton, we were flat broke and had to return to Jasper. Jim had a job as an Engineer on the Railroad and I had to start looking. Ed Neighbor, a local entrepreneur, had his hands in anything and everything that could turn a dollar.

He had bought an old war surplus Studebaker weapon carrier, that had been modified for a freight truck. When I asked him for work, he told me to take the truck and another person to the Athabasca River crossing east of Jasper where a new bridge had recently been built. Our job was to salvage all the bridge timbers we could and haul them to Curly Phillip's boat shed on Pyramid Lake Road. The truck was a nightmare to drive but we finally hauled all the timber he needed for his next project. Ed had made a deal buying the boat shed, a two-story log structure about 25'x40'. Our job was to raise the building on to the timbers and skid it to Ed's property about a quarter mile down the road.

Of special concern was not to twist the building so the chinking would not fall out. As with anything Curly Phillip ever made the building withstood the moving without any problem. Although Curly suffered greatly from asthma, especially when working in the boat shed he continued building boats and canoes which have survived the ages of time. The first pair of skis I owned at the age of five were made by Curly. For years after Curly died, the inverted wooden moulds used to frame the river canoes and boats laid outside the shed as a reminder of his ability

Employed as a millhand at this planer mill at Dunvegan, Alberta, 1950.

and recognition as a boat builder.

Some of Ed Neighbor's other business interest were delivering wood and coal and unloading freight from the railroad. Paydays were unscheduled events and amount of pay was usually decide on by the current balance sheet.

With this insecure and unpredictable employment and the memory of my visit to Edmonton, I decided to go back for two reasons, to see Edie again and look for work. Arriving in Edmonton I shared an apartment with Francis Donnelly and Ken Cook, another Jasper railroader.

After a few days of answering employment ads in the paper I landed a job unloading and dry-piling green frozen planking for a planer mill on the outskirts of the City at the Dunvegan yards on the road to St. Albert. Catching the Calder bus at 6:30 a.m. and walking the last two miles to the mill, piling heavy frozen planks all day and returning to the city after dark left me completely exhausted until it was time to go to the South Side to visit Edie.

Often my visits lasted until the busses and street cars had quit running for the night and I'd have to borrow the price of a taxi fare to get back to the apartment. This routine was wearing me down, keeping me broke and long-term employment unlikely.

Just before Christmas I made the biggest decision of my life to ask Edie to marry me. After walking home in a quiet winter snowfall after midnight Mass, surprised her with a ring. She said yes. During the holiday we visited her parents and answered some very direct questions. My response made me realize I had little to offer at this time. No advanced education, no permanent job, no special qualifications, no bank account, no place to live and the list went on. The clincher came when we told her parents we planned to marry in June. I could sense their concern but being an optimist I was sure things would work out.

Earlier, I had confided in Francis what my intentions were and surprisingly he told me he was having the same thoughts. Lucille was in his plans for the future. One weekend Francis and I were walking the streets of Edmonton and passed a jewellery store on Jasper Avenue. We stopped to window shop and read the sign, "Your Credit Is Fine With Irving Kline." Francis turned to me and said "Let's go and buy Lucille an engagement ring." After a great deal of patience on the part of the salesman, we selected a suitable ring and asked to have it set aside to be picked up later. The salesman required a 10% deposit, this amounted to $25.00. Francis turned to me and asked for a loan and I thanked him for the compliment that I would be so rich.

Then the negotiations with the salesman started. He dropped the deposit to $15.00, we shook our heads, "Okay $10.00?" No. "How about $5.00?" No. "Well, $2.00? The best I can do." Once again Francis turned to me and asked, "Do you have $2.00?" Yes, I did and the deal was sealed. I always thought I had an investment in Lucille first but they were married the following September and still making payments on that ring.

Right after Christmas we caught the train to Jasper where Dad met us at the station and drove us to Athabasca Falls. Edie's first trip to the mountains was memorable. The old Portal Creek Hill without guardrails was a sheet of ice and seemed to her to be heading straight up to the mountain tops. Our holiday was picture perfect. Our moonlight walks on the highway with the glistening cold frosty air and the white shining mountains is a memory that has lasted our lifetime.

To try and meet the June commitment, I stayed in Jasper and Edie returned to Edmonton to her job at Muttart Lumber where she was a Bookkeeping Machine Operator.

Edna had worked and saved for three years and had acquired what was considered at the time desirable to begin married life. She and her creditors had invested in a fur coat, a set of sterling silver, a set of Wearever Aluminum pots and pans, and had her teeth in good shape. The June wedding came before the pots and pans were paid.

The only work I could find was a job on the Section Gang for the C.N.R. at Grantbrook, B.C. just west of the Yellowhead Pass. A bunkhouse was provided but you had to look after your own provisions. The crew was a Section Foreman, two other labourers and myself. All four of us spoke a different language and kept to ourselves. The work was straight forward—checking for broken rails and tamping loose ties, called "gandy-dancing," and keeping the switches clear of snow. I passed the long winter evenings writing letters to Edie making big plans for the future and telling her how much I missed her. Those letters are still cached up in the attic, as well as her's to me and I hope they never surface. They should make writing paper that disintegrates so the decision when to throw them away is not left up to you.

The winter passed with two events highlighting my career as a section hand. One morning we left the bunkhouse which was located about 20 feet from the track, to go to work and noticed the ground and the crossties all broken up. Also, every second bolt that secured the flanges holding the steel rails together was severed on the end that had the nut. On the other rail, the one farthest from us, had exactly the same damage except on the inside. We found out what had happened when we walked to the east switch. One of the freight cars of a train that passed through in the night jumped the track at the switch, and it travelled parallel to the steel rails over the frozen ground and crossties. As it moved along, the wheels had cut off the nuts. When it reached the west end switch, about a half mile distance, it jumped back on the track without causing a derailment. It was scary to think that a freight car had rolled by your bunk on the ground only a few feet away with the rest of the train staying on the tracks with every second bolt cut off for the half mile.

The second event happened west of Grantbrook near the Moosehorn River crossing. A trapper named Johnston was trapping the Moosehorn valley. His cabin was situated above the railroad on the west side of the river. A large black wolf had come down the river past the cabin and on to the railroad track. We were patrolling west on a speeder and as we approached the river crossing, the trapper stepped on to the track and flagged us down. He explained there was a black wolf ahead of us on the track and he would like to catch a ride with us to see if he could get a shot. The section foreman reluctantly agreed, afraid to interrupt his schedule. On a speeder, you sit at right angles to the direction of travel. In this instance I was in front on the right. Johnston seated himself on the opposite side and also in front.

The section foreman got into the spirit of the hunt and wound up the speeder as fast as it would go which is a considerable speed. The snowbanks on each side of the single track were about six feet high. Soon the wolf came into view loping along without a care until he saw the speeder descending upon him.

He picked up speed to try to keep ahead but we were closing in fast. With the snowbanks on either side to keep him from leaving the track, we were now about five feet behind him. What happened next was a surprise to us all. Johnston had reached over the windscreen and pulled the trigger wounding the wolf, who turned with his mouth opened wide snapping at my kneecap. At the same instant the speeder hit with a terrific impact.

The speeder turned a cartwheel and the four of us became airborne landing in the snowbanks. The wolf, still very much alive, landed among us and all five of us in total fear, scattered to safety. Luckily for us the wolf died in the struggle and each of us collected ourselves to survey the damage.

The rest of the crew and I came out of this mishap unscathed but the trapper was not so lucky. Flying through the air, his rifle in hand and landing on it as he fell, he broke his arm. We put the speeder back on the track and returned to the station house where we hailed the next freight to stop and pick up the injured trapper and take him to Jasper.

Working on a section gang was a new experience especially with the language barrier, and when we teamed up with the extra gang it was unbelievable how efficiently work was accomplished. With hand signals, grunts and groans, and synchronized spike driving, steel rails were laid and ties tamped with precision without a word spoken in any language. Entertainment was provided by an Italian worker standing on a pile of railroad ties singing the Roman Catholic High Mass in Latin.

After three months of exposure to this culture I went back to Jasper looking for a different job. I was beginning to feel more secure financially having saved about two hundred dollars and with three months to go before the wedding I knew money wouldn't be an obstacle.

When the first signs of spring came to the Rockies my thoughts nostalgically went back to some of the ski trips I had made to the Tonquin valley and stayed at the Maccarib cabin with Dad, often with school friends. The slopes of Mr. Clitheral were usually ideal for spring skiing. Behind the cabin in a small enclosure was a reminder that once the snow goes this valley becomes the domain of grizzly and man must be ever alert to his presence. A tombstone in the enclosure reads, "Percy Goodair, 1877-1929." Warden Goodair has the sombre distinction of being the only warden killed by a grizzly.

Though still a mystery, some speculate he had gone to cut firewood and had come between a sow and her cub. Apparently he had an axe with him at the time leading to this belief. It happened in September, his horses were out to pasture and with visibility obscured by a snowstorm may have run into a bear on his way to the horses. When his body was found a few days later it was evident he had not been killed outright as he had tried to control the bleeding from a gash in his side.

On a brighter note and with the temptation to go skiing put aside I found a job with the Northland Utilities. Jasper had an independently-owned electric power system that generated its own electricity by hydro power at the mouth of the Astoria River. Standby power was provided by diesel engines located at the power station in town but as the demand for power increased, the combined use of the hydro and diesel-powered generators were working to maximum capacity. The distribution system was being upgraded east of Jasper to Lake Edith and Jasper Park Lodge areas and so I was hired to work as a lineman on reconstructing the power line.

The poles were 35 feet high and made from hard seasoned fir wood. My previous experience in climbing poles was limited to a few months on the telephone crew for the Park. With the poles tapering to about six inches at the top and with the spikes of climbing spurs hardly making an indentation, by the time I'd reach the crossarm I was out of breath, more from fear than exertion. Now I was expected to lean out backwards and with tie-wire, tie the transmission line to the insulator. The thought often crossed my mind that I'd never live to see my wedding day.

June finally arrived and taking leave, I went to Edmonton with Jim Donnelly who was to be my best man. We stayed at the King George hotel and the night before the wedding, the skies opened up with rain, lightning and thunder making me wonder if the heavens were trying to tell me something.

June 9th, 1951 dawned with the storm passed by and everything went according to plan. We were married at St. Alphonsus church by Father Cunningham, with Father Felix Otterson, an old friend from Edie's former parish, St. Anthony's, in attendance. Lucille was Edie's bridesmaid and Edie's father, Joseph Dubord, gave her away. Our families, close relatives and friends numbered approximately eighty. Unknown to me during the ceremony, I was standing on the hem of Edie's wedding dress and everytime she leaned towards me to push me off I returned the push thinking it was her sign of affection. After a buffet lunch at her parents' home, where Father "Fee" proposed the toast to the bride, giving here a rolling pin to keep me in line (which she still has), and cake made and decorated by her mother, Olivina. I borrowed Jim's car and we left for Banff for a week's honeymoon.

It was soon time to go back to our home in Jasper, a house Dad and Mom owned that we rented. At work I had a new assignment. The company had purchased a war surplus electric diesel-powered generating plant which had been used by the U.S. Army in the Philippines. It arrived on a railroad flatcar all covered with rust. When the boss said he expected to have it operational by fall I didn't believe it. The unit was unloaded and a fellow worker, Jim Yoeman and I started cleaning the exterior, which seemed to take forever.

While this took place, Frank Owen was busy preparing the footing to place it on in the power house. The overall size measured about 25 feet long, 6 feet wide and 7 feet high and must have weighed ten to twelve tons. The footing was a block of cement about half again as big as the unit, located below ground level. Once in place on the base the more detailed work began.

The whole machine had to be dismantled, cleaned, adjusted and put back together. There were six huge cylinders and pistons at least 16 inches in diameter and a sixteen-foot crankshaft about 8 inches in diameter. The bearings were made of babbitt and to finally get everything lined up perfectly took the skill of a machinist. When finished, compressed air was used to start it running. For years it produced the extra electric energy needed by the town.

By the time this work was finished I had absorbed all the grease and oil and smell of diesel exhaust I wanted. At home one night I cautiously told Edie I'd had enough and would she agree if I changed jobs. The question was, "Well, what would you like to do?" A very simple answer, go back to the bush, and Edie's response, "Why not?"

REINSTATED AS A PARK WARDEN

I went to see the Chief Warden and asked it he would take me back as a Park Warden. The answer was, "Yes, on one condition, you go back to the Brazeau and pick up where you left off two years ago." If I'd agree, I should be ready to leave the next week, as it was already September.

Louis Joachim, an Indian packer, was standing by with nine pack horses to move us in with one trip only. I gladly agreed and ran home to tell Edie the plan. We really didn't know where to start at such short notice.

The first question was money. We needed to buy eight months supply of groceries, winter clothing and suitable footwear and we only had my month's cheque from the power company to meet our current commitments. I approached Bill Robinson at Robinson's Groceries and Drygoods and asked if he would extend me credit for about $500. He said, sure, no problem, and I immediately was overcome with a fear of being committed to a large debt.

The second thing, Edie suspected she had just become pregnant so visited Dr. O'Hagan who told her, yes, and go ahead, everything will be all right. It took a few days to convince myself I'd done the right thing but we were on our way and couldn't look back.

I made up the grocery list with all staple foods in bulk units consisting mostly of flour, sugar, beans, macaroni, rice, dried fruit, canned chicken haddie of the sea, Lipton's chicken noodle soup, bacon, canned butter, coffee, and similar items on which I had survived during my previous winters in the bush. We bought Edie warm bush clothes and suitable footwear and socks for horseback riding and snowshoeing.

Packing in our winter supplies over Nigel Pass enroute to the Brazeau Warden District.

We met the deadline and Lucille and Francis, who had just got married early September and were moving to Jasper, where Francis had transferred back to work for the railroad, took over the house. They would use our furniture, and at the same time we had storage space in the basement for our other personal belongings.

Everything, including the horses, was trucked out to Camp Parker, just south of Columbia Icefields. The packs were made up and the next morning we crossed Nigel Pass in a snowstorm and down into the Brazeau valley where the weather was more pleasant.

This day was a "First" for Edie—her first to ride a saddle horse and her first to travel into the mountains for the eighteen mile, seven hour trip to Brazeau Lake cabin. When she dismounted at the cabin her legs gave way, but her recovery soon allowed her to cook supper while Louis and I unpacked and looked after the horses.

The provisions had to be divided, a portion going to each of the seven cabins on the district to ensure very little food had to be transported during the winter from location to location. With the packs remade we started downriver for Isaac Creek and another long day for saddle-sore Edie. Since the day the old cabin at Isaac was built, a toilet had never been constructed but with winter coming, Edie considered this a priority so we built one out of upright split logs.

We made a quick trip to Southesk and Cairn cabins in perfect autumn weather to provision these cabins. The night we spent at Cairn cabin was another memorable night for Edie. A packrat had moved in and the smell of his presence made her sick but there was no way to find out where he was nested so I could get rid of him.

We went to bed and after I had fallen asleep, Edie woke me and asked what was that noise she heard. I listened and said it was the packrat tamping his feet. She insisted she wanted to have a look at it so I handed her the flashlight and I reached for my rifle and put a shell in the chamber. I instructed her to turn the light on and when she located the rat's eyes, hold the light on them and I would shoot it for her.

The rat was on the top log just below the roof and I pulled the trigger. A blinding flash of light came out of the gun barrel and the noise in the cabin temporarily deafened us. Edie dropped the flashlight and by the time I picked it up and looked around for the rat, all I could locate were tufts of grey hair floating around in the cabin and a blood spot on the roof where the bullet had disintegrated the rat and put a hole through the roof. She still had no idea what a rat looked like.

For the last few days Edie had been violently ill, and complained of the smell of coffee brewing, and the packrat smell that permeated the old cabins. We hadn't planned on coming back out with Louis but thought we should see the doctor again. We knew she was pregnant but didn't know anything about morning sickness. Our concern was the strength she would need for hiking and snowshoeing during the winter, but Doc O'Hagan reassured us it would pass and she was in good health.

I knew the Brazeau valley could support horses as it had lots of meadows and mild temperatures in wintertime but the Park Service had a policy all horses must winter in the Athabasca valley. We bought two old horses, Black Hawk and Peanuts for twenty-five dollars, trucked them to Poboktan Creek headquarters and rode them up to Waterfalls, and across Poboktan Pass which is 7500 feet altitude.

Peanuts and Black Hawk.

By now it had snowed at the higher elevations and ice was forming on the water-crossings. I would sometimes have to lead Edie's horse across snowbanks and half frozen creeks where all she could do was hang on to the pommel as the horse jumped back onto firmer ground. Sometimes she had to get off while Peanuts had to be half-skidded across flooded stream beds. She

(Above) A winter patrol leaving Isaac Creek. Edie riding Peanuts, Black Hawk packing and Smoky and I walking.
(Below) Smoky in harness hauling stakes to make a safe winter route across Brazeau Lake.

has often said that's where she learned what good care I took of her on this her first winter trip and would trust me no matter what could happen in the coming months.

Once over the Pass, it was a warm, balmy fall all over again and we rode the horses without difficulty all over the district. With the exception of Edie's morning sickness, which seemed to last all day and caused her to dream of the days at the farm in the garden eating fresh, dewy peas picked from the vine, and carrots straight from the ground, and succulent strawberries and all the wonderful potatoes and fresh meat and milk. . .it was a far cry from the reality of macaroni, chicken haddie, elk meat, beans, and canned milk, which was all she had to look forward to all winter.

Edie spent a lot of time browsing through the old Blue Rib-

Crossing Brazeau Lake on the winter trail. Poboktan Mountain is in the background.

bon Cookbooks that were left in the cabins, and trying to make palatable meals with the somewhat bland foods I had hurriedly selected for our staple diet for the winter. She tried her hand at baking bread and biscuits but soon said she'd leave that to me as I was more experienced in wilderness cooking.

Back at the Brazeau cabin we made preparations for our return trip to Jasper for Christmas. A couple of depressing days were spent washing clothes in a 25 pound powdered-milk can with a plunger. The steam from heating water on the stove, wringing out clothes by hand, hanging them on lines strung in the cabin, or bringing them in frozen from outside, all made for a few very uncomfortable days until everything was dry.

I had staked out a trail across the now frozen Brazeau Lake to mark a safe crossing and make the trip shorter when the time came to be on our way. I had made a dog sleigh and harness for our dog Smoky to haul our personal effects, extra clothing and food. It was easier for me to break a snowshoe trail over the pass without a pack on my back.

Our return trip to the district after Christmas was difficult. I bought two more dogs and planned to run a three-dog dog team using the same sleigh I'd built before Christmas. I was encouraged to try out a dog team after knowing that Charlie Matheson, an old time warden on the Brazeau in previous years had some success with a five-dog dog team.

Dog food is always a problem and when Charlie was asked by the Chief Warden how he intended to feed his dogs, he replied, tongue in cheek, "A sheep a day, Sir." The Chief Warden wasn't impressed, and knowing Charlie, it probably was a sheep a day.

I left the highway with my three dogs and sleigh loaded with the condiments and special delight foods that I hadn't felt were necessary when we stocked our provisions in the fall. These foods included peanut butter and jam, chocolate bars and trail mix to complement the bland diet and make meals more satisfying. Elk meat and beans just didn't have much appeal to Edie in her condition. I planned to reach Waterfall cabin and return to Athabasca Falls where she waited.

The first problem I encountered was the order I had the dogs hooked up. Smoky, having been over the trail was in my mind the lead dog, but there was no way he would track and pull. I moved Barney to lead and put Smoky as the wheel dog. Barney, half wolf, half husky, was born to lead and away we went until we came to switchbacks on the trail.

With all the power up front, Smoky didn't have the strength to keep the sleigh on the trail on a sharp corner. The traces pulled him to the inside corner and into the deep snow causing the sleigh to follow and tip.

For mile after mile I hoped Smoky would try harder but I finally turned him loose. With Barney and Buck pulling a heavier load than planned and the snow getting deeper as I climbed, when I reached Harrigan Falls I stopped. Unloading the sleigh and caching my supplies I turned back to the highway arriving at Athabasca Falls in the dark.

Harrigan Falls on Poboktan Creek was named after Mona Matheson, Charlie's wife. Mona and her sister, Agnes Harrigan came to Canada from Trinidad in 1908 and to Jasper in 1927. They worked as Brewster trail hands at Medicine and Maligne Lakes. Mona married Charlie in 1930 and Agnes married Mark Truxler the same year. Mark was a park employee for twenty years at Miette Hot Springs and the East Gate. Mona Peak, at the top end of Medicine Lake, and Mona Lake, a short day hike from the chalet at Maligne Lake, are named after Mona.

The next morning, this time with Edie, we were back on the trail. The going was better and we reached the Waterfall cabin. Smoky stayed behind and found a new home with Art Sculthorpe, who later had the misfortune of losing his hand in the wardens planer mill on the Whirlpool River.

The following morning I came back to pick up the cache at the Falls and then broke trail towards the Pass. When I returned to Waterfalls, Dad had arrived, anxious to see how we were making out and he decided to accompany us to the Brazeau cabin. The next day we made it to the junction of the Jonas Shoulder trail and had to make camp. After starting a fire and leaving Edie to look after it, Dad and I broke trail to the foot of the pass and

Crossing Poboktan Pass with Barney and Buck in harness.

returned to the campsite. I had built the fire at the foot of an alpine spruce tree. The pitch on the tree caught fire which helped to fuel the fire. Without a tarp or bedroll we spent the night seated in front of the fire on spruce boughs.

The next day we crossed the Pass and stopped at Poboktan shelter, where Edie had another cooking lesson. Water boils fast and hard at this high altitude, but with rarefied air pressure food takes twice as long to cook. On to the Brazeau Headquarters the following morning, we arrived at noon glad to be home. Blisters and snowshoe sickness (mal de raquette) would now have time to heal.

The weather turned bad after Dad left for Athabasca Falls and the temperature dropped to 50 degrees below. It was a good time to build some much needed furniture for the cabin and make it more homey—a pots and pans cupboard instead of hanging them on the wall, a kitchen cupboard to store dishes and food stuffs with a counter to prepare food, and a wash stand. Edie added a bright touch by making curtains out of tea towels.

When the weather warmed we headed down river towards Isaac Creek stopping at Arete Shelter for a couple of days. About four miles below the Brazeau cabin we heard the tinkling of Peanut's brass bell and went over to look at the horses. They were wintering well with lots of feed available.

We spent about a week at Isaac Creek, where I shot my third wolf. I made day patrols to see if anyone had been in the valley since Christmas but found no evidence.

You could always depend on catching a Dolly Varden out of the river so one afternoon we went fishing. We heard wolves howling in the distance up the river but paid little attention to them. Finally Edie hooked on to about a four pound fish. While trying to land it we heard the wolves hunting and it sounded like they had pulled down some game. I asked Edie to hurry so we could go see what had happened. She landed the fish and after a short walk up the river we located an elk kill.

The elk was located in a small clearing in the heavy timber. The wolves left the carcass when we arrived but circled around us in and out of the trees. Edie and I sat on the elk back to back while I tried to get a shot away. Finally the wolves got tired of waiting for us to leave and they continued downriver. As they left we counted 15 animals and for sometime afterwards could hear them howling in the distance. We picked up our fish and returned to the cabin for supper.

The next day we moved back to the Arete shelter after a very difficult start with the dogs. Buck had gotten loose. For some reason, ever since I had picked him up at the train station he wouldn't come near anyone. I had bought him from a kennel in Edson where he must have been treated poorly as he didn't trust anyone. Once he was packed or in a sleigh harness he was the most capable work dog but once loose he was very difficult to catch. He would never leave but kept his distance. To catch him, Edie would fall back on the trail and as he passed her to catch up to the sleigh she would pounce on him and hold him until he was harnessed.

That morning there was no way he'd let us catch him so I had to pull the sleigh with Barney. About a mile up the trail I set a wolf snare. When I heard Buck yelp I knew he was caught and put him back to work. It was strange to see the transformation in him as soon as he was in harness eager to be back in the traces. His ears perked up, and with his tail curled high over his back, every ounce of his strength went into pulling the sleigh.

We stopped for the night at Arete cabin intending to push through to the Brazeau cabin in the morning. Supper consisted of a can of "bully beef" and macaroni. During the night Edie became violently ill which I expected was an early case of morning sickness so I went back to bed after looking after her. It wasn't long until I had to jump out of bed and head out the door to lose my evening meal. We took turns being sick and comforting one another hoping we would maintain enough strength to survive. Canned food subject to freezing and thawing was a possible source of food poisoning.

We blamed the bully beef for our condition and we were thankful we were still alive in the morning. We took that day to regain our strength but with the added comforts at Brazeau waiting for us, we moved the next morning.

Not thinking very clearly yet, I overlooked one very important detail when travelling with a dog team. On the back of the sleigh is a haulback rope about 15 feet long. When going down hill it is used to keep the sleigh from running up on the dogs and injuring them. When climbing it provides assistance if the trail is packed and your snowshoes slide backwards. For Edie, it was a great help when she was tired and didn't want to fall behind.

Normal practise when preparing for departure is to tie the haulback back to a stump, tree, or corner post of the cabin before hooking up the dogs. When it's time to go the dogs are in a frenzy to travel and this morning was no exception. Overlooking step one, to secure the sleigh, I hooked up the dogs and when I straightened up the sleigh went by me in a blur. Instead of taking the trail Barney cut down to the river and once on the ice, hit a loping stride and disappeared. I knew if they didn't fall into open water they would enter the canyon and eventually stop at the foot of a frozen waterfall about three miles up the valley.

We left the cabin with Edie travelling on the trail and I went looking for the dogs. I found them where I expected and they greeted me with a look that suggested why had I taken so long. Back-tracking down the canyon until I could climb up to the trail above, caught up to Edie and she also wondered why I had taken so long. I was exhausted so the question remained unanswered.

Back once again at our headquarters and in telephone communication with the warden office, I reported to the Chief Warden. He asked me if I would like to come to town for about a month and work in the main valley replacing some of the wardens who were taking annual leave. It sounded like a great idea and a timely offer.

By now Edie had outgrown most of her winter clothing especially her parka. She had a hard time getting the zipper to close over her tummy. Our trip out was uneventful although we took precautions to travel early in the morning and avoid the possibility of avalanches that crossed the trail just below Poboktan shelter. The Pass was a winter wonderland and a joy to experience.

Edie snowshoeing to town to await the arrival of our first baby, spring of 1952.

CHAPTER

10

A SPRING BREAK IN
THE ATHABASCA VALLEY

RRIVING in Jasper in early March we rented a cabin at Bud
Bolie's Bungalows. It was an opportunity to entertain
and visit our friends and relatives and make preparations for the birth of the baby expected in early June.

With the approach of warm weather the elk slaughter was
finished for the year. The meat and hides had to be shipped while
still frozen. It was also time to start recovering the poison baits
that by now had taken their toll of wolves, coyotes, eagles,
cougar, and foxes.

In retrospect, there was such a contradiction in National
Parks policy of game management during these years, yet the
wardens treated it as a condition of their employment. One day
we would be out killing elk, shooting wolves, poisoning small
mammals and birds and the next day we were on patrol ensuring
no one entered the park with an unsealed firearm or caught fishing in closed waters. We would spend hours glassing the park
boundary waiting for some unsuspecting hunter to cross the
boundary so we could charge him. One of my assignments that
spring was to man the east park gate during the dark hours and
record the vehicle traffic as it entered and left the park. If the next
day there was evidence of poaching in the park, we might have a
lead on possible violators.

Poachers seemed to enjoy playing games with some of the
park wardens. In the fall of 1946 when Dad and I were packing
supplies into the Brazeau, we had just ridden out on the flats at
the headquarter cabin when we heard a rifle shot. On the open
hillside above us were three goats running and while we watched
one fell and lay still. We pulled the packs from the horses and
went down river to a game trail we knew came off the hillside

where we had seen the goats. We saw a man's foot print on the trail leading to a meadow near the Park boundary. Dad and I climbed up to the goat hoping to recover a slug that could be used as evidence and give us reasonable and probable grounds to cross the boundary to the hunting camp and seize any firearms. A Park warden had all the powers of a police officer and under the authority of the National Parks Act, could search, seize or arrest without a warrant when there were reasonable and probable grounds.

The goat had been hit low behind the front shoulders and the bullet had passed right through the body. We left the goat on the hillside hoping that the perpetrator might return to recover the trophy.

The next morning a hunter rode up to the cabin and sat with us out in the yard. Soon he glanced the hillside with his field glasses. He commented he had heard a rifle shot yesterday afternoon and wanted to know if there had been some shooting in the Park. With the dead goat lying clearly in view, the answer was affirmative. It was hard to keep from accusing him of the shooting but we had no evidence. If we hadn't delayed in pulling the packs off the horses we might have met him coming off the ridge.

In April I went back to the district alone as Edie was well along in her pregnancy and snowshoeing would have been difficult. When I arrived at Waterfalls cabin, Tom Ross, the Sunwapta district warden, was doing some renovations so I decided to lay over a day and give him a hand. I received a call from the Chief Warden during the day asking me if I would like to transfer to the Rocky River district. The advantages of moving was welcome considering the access to the Jacques Lake cabin was much easier and shorter than getting to the Brazeau district. I phoned Edie the good news and future plans took a new turn.

I went to Jacques Lake and talked to Warden Clarence Wilkins and took inventory of material and supplies I thought would be needed to make the cabin more habitable. Returning to town, approval was given to go ahead. The plywood for partitions was cut and bundled into packable packhorse size and cupboards were built and dismantled for packing. By mid-May there was enough snow left for the dog sleigh to run so I hauled the linoleum floor covering to the cabin.

It was too early for the horses so I asked for help to rebuild the phone line from Jacques Lake to Rocky Forks. A trail hand from town came out and we began working our way towards Rocky Forks. To save time backtracking each evening to a cabin we carried a light camping outfit and set up a camp near where we would work for a couple of days as we moved on up the trail.

When we were within a couple of miles of each cabin we stayed there instead of sleeping under a tarp on the edge of the trail. In about two weeks the line was up and working well so it was back to town for the horses. Working out of the Beaver Lake cabin I would take three packhorse loads of material into Jacques Lake and return to the Beaver cabin at night. Eventually everything I needed was at Jacques Lake and I started the renovations.

At last on June 4, 1952 the long awaited phone call came telling me Edie was in labour in the hospital. I went to town immediately but by the time I arrived, our baby girl had arrived. It had been quite an experience. Labour had started during the night so at dawn her sister, Lucille, with whom she had been staying, walked with her to the hospital. It was a cold chilly one mile walk and when they arrived they were told no beds were left. All available beds were occupied by army personnel, even the cots set up in the hallways.

Ever since the war, the Jasper area had been the training grounds for mountaineering. The first to arrive in the early 40's were the Lovett Scouts from Scotland. They were a tough bunch of men and the training to which they were subjected was almost suicidal. Poor equipment, heavy packs and exposure to danger-ous mountain hazards all took their toll. Their bivouac campsites could be found throughout the park. Supplies and equipment would surface on the mountainsides and glaciers after the snow melt receded. Those who survived the training were shipped to Salerno, Italy where most were killed in that famous battle. After the Lovett Scouts came the English and Canadian troops and to this day the training continues.

Why so many of the troops were hospitalized that day we don't know. The only privacy Edie was given was the doctor's office and the only place to lay down was his desk, with a thin pad for a mattress. With all those men just outside her door, she felt very inhibited making loud birthing noises. Finally she was moved to the delivery room where Dr. O'Hagan had to use tongs to help with a very difficult birth. Our poor little girl had black and blue bruises on her head and ears, and her mother, very sore arms from fighting the straps that held her tight as she fought to give birth. The one bright light was Edie ended up with the best room in the house, as the maternity ward was also full. This room was called the Gold Room, usually reserved for visiting priest and other V.I.P.'s, where both mother and daughter were given tender loving care by the Sisters and other nurses. They stayed at the hospital for about ten days and the room became a place where all our friends and relatives gathered to visit. We named our little dark-haired girl, Deborah Marie.

As soon as Edie's recovery was assured, I left for the Brazeau district with Warden Norman Hooper to pack out my personal possessions and look for Peanuts and Black Hawk. The horses had wintered on Job Creek Flats and I got my first glimpse of Peanuts' foal, which we named Popcorn. Back at the highway we trucked the horses to Medicine Lake. I stopped in Jasper for a visit and went on to Jacques Lake to prepare the cabin for the family.

By the first week in July, Edie had recovered her strength and I went to town to pick her up. On July 3rd her Dad had passed away in Edmonton, and she was in a quandary whether to go to the funeral or move to Jacques Lake. After talking to her mother, she decided to go to Jacques Lake as it was crucial that if she would successfully nurse the baby, she should get settled as soon as possible in her own home.

CHAPTER

11

JACQUES LAKE
OUR NEW FAMILY HOME

WITH the horses at Beaver cabin at the upper end of Medicine Lake, I went to town and returned with Edie and Debbie. To save a five-mile packhorse trip around Medicine Lake I borrowed a boat with the idea I would move the family up the lake by water. Medicine Lake is a lake of mystery. At times it rises to a height of 50 to 60 feet and then drops to only a river channel running through the lake bed. Evidence of this fluctuating level is whirlpools of water at the lower end of the lake where the water disappears below the ground. There is no hard evidence to say what controls the discharge from the lake which can be almost overnight.

Interestingly, Medicine Lake is in Ripley's "Believe It Or Not." During winter when the lake is frozen over and covered with snow, if you are skiing up the lake, the sun casts your shadow to your left side and the sun reflecting off the mountains casts your shadow to your right side. According to Ripley, this is the only place in the world where the sun casts a shadow on both sided of you at the same time.

The day we moved the lake was low. The trip started off well but the farther we travelled upstream the shallower the water. Soon the river divided into a number of tributaries, many of them too shallow for the boat. It was an afternoon of trial and error looking for a channel with enough water to float the boat. Soon I had to disembark into soft mud and pull the boat, often with the keel dragging bottom.

Anyone watching this performance from up on the mountainside wouldn't believe what he was seeing. We were thankful Debbie remained quite happy during this strenuous voyage. The end of the lake never seemed to get any closer as we changed directions so many times but finally we made it to the Beaver cabin for a well-earned rest.

We saddled up the next morning and started up the trail. One of our possessions was a kitten someone convinced us we should have to hunt for the many mice in the meadow around the cabin. It had survived the boat trip and now it's mode of travel was the baby's bassinet, a top-pack on one of the packhorses. The bassinet swayed back and forth with every step the horse took. The kitten dug its claws into the mattress and braced itself from being tossed around. Another unusual item we brought in was Edie's treadle Singer Sewing Machine which would come in handy for the many things we could sew. We even had a rocking chair.

Debbie was carried in a sling in our arms, and it being a very hot day, suffered a severe heat rash by the time we reached the cabin. The cabin was in the throws of renovation and we planned to stay in the equipment shed for a few days. The first thing we unpacked was the kitten. What a sight as it tried to walk! Its motion from the long hours on horseback were quite comical as it staggered around the yard. She soon recovered and explored around her new home. Top priority was to finish the cabin renovations and move in before Edie's Mom and brother Mark would arrive for a visit after the funeral. When I knew Mark was coming I asked if he would bring his old 30-06 army rifle so Edie would have a firearm at the cabin while I was away.

Drinking water had to be carried from a spring located across a foot bridge on the opposite side of the creek flowing out of the lake. The distance from the cabin to the water supply was about 300 yards and the big hazard was moose. The meadow in front of the cabin was a favourite feeding yard for moose and often when we went for water, especially during the rutting season, they would chase us. In my absence, sometimes for days, Edie had to fetch the water and outrun a moose at the same time.

An early morning visitor to the salt lick.

The purpose of the rifle was for her to fire two or three shots into the air, hoping the moose would scare and leave the meadow. Her greatest concern was leaving the baby in the cabin while she made a dash for the water and not being able to get back to the cabin. My concern was not to shoot a moose as the next problem would be a dead moose attracting grizzlies.

The plan worked reasonably well except on one occasion. Edie stood on the porch, fired the rifle to clear the meadow of moose and a big, old bull moose took exception to being interrupted from his feeding, or maybe the noise made him mad. He entered the lake and ran back and forth in the shallow water, snorting and bellowing and thrashing and churning the water with his antlers and front feet. Edie was completely unnerved as she shakingly hung on to the corner post of the porch, and didn't go for water that day.

As soon as Debbie grew a little stronger Edie wanted to make a trip with me to the Rocky River and Rocky Forks cabin. We hadn't resolved the problem of carrying Debbie when on the trail so we made a mossbag designed along the lines used by the Indians. We cut a piece of plywood about a foot longer than Debbie, padded with a piece from an old mouton lamb overcoat Edie's mother had given her to make a bunting bag for the baby for the coming winter. We made the outer covering out of canvas, attaching straps at the back for the carrier. We trimmed it with bright red from a flag and laced it with leather shoelaces. The inner bag was also from the old coat. A head band around the upper part of the board and across her forehead kept her head from flopping around. We accomplished all this with our handy sewing machine and speed sew.

The first time we put her in her new cradle board she protested loudly until we gave her the freedom of her hands and stuck a soother in her mouth. Then we went for a trial walk, Edie walking anxiously behind me with Debbie on my back. Debbie immediately quieted down, which alarmed Edie. We quickly put her down and checked her out, and in the process woke her up from a nap. The crying started all over again until she was back on my back rocked to the rhythm of my walking. When she was awake, she'd blow bubbles and gurgle at whichever one of us was walking facing her.

The shoulder straps for the mossbag were designed to carry the baby high on our shoulders and would allow a person to ride a horse.

On our first trip to the Rocky we stayed a few days at the Grizzly cabin and made some changes in the cabin to make it more comfortable for us all. From the two small bunks I made

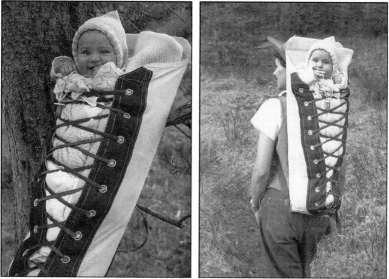

(Left) Debbie enjoying her mossbag at three months of age.
(Right) Edie and Debbie near the Grizzly cabin enroute to Rocky Forks cabin.

one wider for a double, and with the other I enclosed it with a railing for a crib.

When we arrived at the Rocky Forks cabin, we were met by Norman Hooper who had come over from the Brazeau district for a visit. This was Norm's first year as a warden and it gave him an opportunity to talk to me and exchange information I had about the Brazeau valley and what he could expect when the fall hunting season opened along the boundary.

When we returned to Jacques Lake cabin I dug a water well near the cabin hoping to resolve the inconvenience of carrying water such a great distance and make life easier for Edie when I left for a couple of weeks on game patrol. We struck water at 16 feet with an adequate water supply but it went dry a couple of days before I left for the Medicine Tent River boundary patrol so it was back to the spring for water.

The Park boundary was the height of land between the Cardinal River in the Province and the Medicine Tent River. It was a favourite area for hunting sheep. The high alpland basin northwest of Mt. Cardinal was a favourite spot to poach sheep out of the Park. It was difficult to approach from the Park side up the canyon and into the basin without being seeing by a poacher watching from in the basin but it did discourage some hunters. Word would spread that a warden was around and accomplished as much as trying to catch someone after he had shot a trophy.

After the boundary patrol and before the horses were turned out to winter pasture I established a temporary shelter between Rocky Forks and the Grizzly cabin and another shelter between Grizzly cabin and Jacques Lake. These emergency shelters would serve for an overnight layover or rest area en route between cabins. The cabins were adequately stocked and all perishable canned milk and baby food was cached in metal containers and submerged in water springs to keep from freezing. The labels would separate from the cans and sometimes the supper menu for Debbie was uncertain until the cans were opened.

On the first winter patrol up the Rocky River, the dogs were packed instead of using the sleigh. With Debbie in the mossbag on my back and Edie carrying a day pack, it would have been difficult to look after the dogsleigh. The packs I made for the dogs were large enough to carry all the essentials for the baby and some survival supplies. The advantage of packing dogs if the snow isn't too deep is they become very adept at carrying a load equal in weight to sixty percent of their body weight.

We travelled at a good pace and found it unnecessary to overnight at the halfway shelters on this trip. The twelve mile distance between the cabins made for a long day but the comfort of a cabin over a teepee provided the encouragement to keep going. The Grizzly cabin had a mouse problem and kept us busy trying to catch as many as possible. At night after the lamp was out, we would lay awake listening to them scurrying about and in the morning we'd assess the damage. We had placed our shoepack insoles under the heater to dry overnight. It was humorous to see that the only insoles all fluffed up by the mice as they helped themselves to the wool to line their nests, were Edie's. They must have turned up their noses at mine because they weren't touched. Debbie slept in a bunting bag with white rabbit fur around her hood and every night small sections of this fur disappeared. These thieves in the night never woke her up.

Crossing the Rocky River above Grizzly cabin was always a problem. Unless it was a severely cold winter the river stayed open and had to be waded to get across. A pair of hip waders hanging in a

Barney packed and ready to go. Note the swede saw in the pack. Chainsaws were yet to come into vogue.

tree were used to cross and recross the open water until everything and everybody was on the other side.

The Rocky Forks cabin is located in one of the nicest setting of any cabin in the mountains. On the edge of a large meadow with mountains all around and a good source of water nearby, it's not hard to spend some time exploring in many different directions within a day's patrol.

The weather turned cold and it began to snow so we decided to move out in case a storm moved in and covered our packed snowshoe trail home. We made it to the Grizzly in one day and laid over the next before continuing on to Jacques Lake. By now the storm had settled in and when we reached the halfway shelter the next afternoon, we decided to spend the night. With a large open fire we were comfortable and Debbie was mesmerized by the flames and sparks dancing about. The night passed without incident and we left for Jacques Lake soon after daylight.

What had been a stack of neatly folded cloth diapers that fit nicely in the dog packs was now a heap of frozen, odd-shaped balls we could hardly fit into the same packs. The Indians in the olden days were smarter than us when it came to resolving the diaper problem. Dry moss stored in trees on the usual route travelled was used to line the baby's mossbag and disposed of after being soiled. The biological composition of moss prevented diaper rash, so they say.

Back at Jacques Lake cabin one of the first tasks was to thaw out the frozen diapers and this process intensified the aroma before they could be washed. Washday was an all day affair. Water was hauled to the equipment shed and heated. I had packed in an antique washing machine, which had been given to us by Edie's mother. It was a square wooden tub on legs with a concave bottom. The top section was a corrugated wooden rocker that corresponded with the tub bottom. The tub was filled with hot water and detergent added with a batch of clothes. The rocker part was attached on each side of the tub and the pivot arm was rocked back and forth by hand over the clothes between the two sections. After the wash cycle, the clothes were wrung out in a wringer attached at one end of the tub. The clothes were rinsed in another tub and hung outside and brought in a few at a time to dry by the stove.

Washing detergent was relatively new and we had brought in a case of "Surf" in the fall. Surf really cleaned the clothes but had a serious effect on Edie's hand. Her hands became red, inflamed, cracked and bleeding, so badly that we went to Jasper to see the Doctor. He advised no more detergent and start using Maple Leaf Soapflakes. We returned with medication and a supply of Maple

Leaf on the dog sleigh and Edie's hands healed.

One way we could keep in touch with the outside world was with a small battery-powered radio. With an antenna high above the trees and pointing to the prairies, we'd receive good radio reception. CBC from Edmonton or Red Deer came in loud and clear. One morning Edie heard of a contest about the use of Maple Leaf Soapflakes. She entered this contest telling how we had to snowshoe twelve miles with the baby in a mossbag on our backs in the dead of winter and on into town to see the Doctor, and how thankful she was that this gentle soap had relieved her painful hands. About a month later, her letter was read on the Cross-Canada program and she received a $25.00 prize.

One evening I stepped outside the cabin door to look around and to the southwest the sky was glowing red like the last rays of sun were shining on the clouds. It was way beyond sunset and in the wrong direction from where Northern Lights would be seen. I called to Edie to come and look, and we watched for a long time until the sky became a pink glow. The next morning I phoned the warden office and spoke to Harry Driver, the office warden. He told me the main lodge at Jasper Park Lodge had burned. It had been built in 1923 with the distinction of being the largest log structure ever built under one roof. Over the years it had been oiled and varnished many times which probably made it burn with great intensity. The blaze must have been spectacular for us to have seen the glow. From the cabin at the 5000 foot level we had been looking over the top of Mt. Sirdar, 9000 feet high and the Colin Range with a distance of 15 air miles between us and the fire.

Early in the summer of 1948 when I had spent time at Jacques Lake with Louis Reese we had a visit from Warden Frank Bryant. Frank had arrived from the Beaver Cabin with Major Woods, the Park Superintendent and camped on the lakeshore. Frank was probably the most exemplary warden to have worked in Jasper and was an inspiring role model. He spoke precise English, wore his uniform with dignity, was always inquisitive and sat his horse with authority. This was the image he left with me as he rode away from the cabin enroute to the highway.

The route he selected was to climb above Jacques Lake to the lower north slope of Mt. Sirdar to the headwaters of Dromore Creek. From there he went over Merlin Pass to Nashan Creek and then into Jacques Pass following the watershed to the highway just north of the Athabasca bridge on the East Highway. Soon after his departure it began to rain and when I inquired a couple of days later how the trip went, the word I got was it was tough. To me, that meant it was really bad and I intended someday to go have a look.

Jim Donnelly had come to pay us a visit and I suggested we make a horse patrol and try to follow Warden Bryant's old trail. There was no sign of any trail leaving the lake so I headed in the general direction of Mt. Sirdar. It was a two thousand foot climb to the summit before descending into Dromore Creek and most of the time we were in heavy timber and windfall. The climb into Merlin Pass was another two thousand feet before dropping into Nashan Creek. I found an old campsite near the creek that I was later told was one of Warden Alex Nellis' stop-overs when he came up from the Snaring cabin, went down Nashan Creek and back to the highway by way of the Rocky River.

At this point I estimated we were about half way to the highway with no sign of a trail to follow so we turned back, arriving at Jacques Lake late in the evening.

Christmas, 1952 was nearing and we made plans to go to town. The weather was exceptionally cold so we were concerned with taking Debbie on the trail. To ensure she wouldn't be cold, we cut holes in a comforter for shoulder straps to completely enclose the mossbag, with just a little breathing space for her face. A handwarmer, about the size of a flashlight, generating heat by burning vapours from a small amount of white gas, was placed at her feet. The baby bottle of milk had to be kept reasonably warm so I place it inside my shirt against my stomach. After some short distance test runs close to the cabin we were satisfied the trip to town was possible.

One memory that haunts me is when we left for town, I struck out across the middle of the lake which I assumed would be frozen hard in this cold spell. There was some open water at the outlet, which I expected and skirted around. When we reached the upper end of the lake I could see mist rising in the cold air from water kept open by warmer water springs. In extreme cold weather some of these air holes freeze over temporarily with a thin coating of ice and light snow makes them undetectable. We managed to avoid these dangerous areas and when we reached the safety of the shore, I thought how foolish it had been to cross the lake under these conditions. The thought of stepping into a hidden air hole and all the heartache it would have caused, has stayed with me always and I thank God it didn't happen.

After Christmas I took holidays and we went to Edmonton to visit Edie's family. It finally struck home that her father had really passed away. Concern was expressed about our lifestyle in the wilderness and we tried to explain that there were many wonderful experiences to enjoy.

12

SKI-MOUNTAINEERING
SEARCH AND RESCUE:
A NEW ROLE FOR PARK WARDENS

W E returned to Jacques Lake after our holiday feeling very much that this was our home and a great way of life. Dad Camp came to visit us on his holidays. Debbie was standing and trying to walk so we made her a playpen where she could play safely. Snow conditions were settled so Dad and I left Edie and the baby for a week's patrol to look around Rocky Forks. We saw seven elk on the slopes of Climax Mountain and tracks of a large pack of wolves that had come down the Medicine Tent River.

Early that spring Chief Warden Pete Brodie phoned to say they were selecting a few wardens to attend a Regional ski-mountaineering school and would I be interested. Park administrators were beginning to realize that the Parks would soon experience a rapid increase in ski activities with the added responsibility of search and rescue. A winter road was pushed into the Marmot Basin area and access was by Bombardier Snowmobile. An army quonset hut had been erected for a chalet and soon a steady increase of skiers began to visit the area.

The ski school was to last six weeks and we would be training in Jasper, Banff and Yoho. I agreed to participate and made plans to move the family to Jasper. By now we were expecting

The original Marmot Basin ski chalet. Skiers are Jim Donnelly, Maryanne Camp and Bill Hornseth.

our second child and it would be better if Edie and Debbie were closer to help if needed. I had built a small suite in the basement of Dad's house that now was occupied by Maryanne and Frank Deagle, who were recently married. We moved into the suite a few days before I had to leave and our first dinner guest was Noel Guardener, the course instructor.

Noel Guardener was employed by the Park Service as a technical advisor to the engineers who were surveying and designing the proposed highway through Rogers Pass. Noel was an avid ski mountaineer and self-taught in the technical qualities of snow structure and hazards of avalanches.

The wardens selected for the course were: from Banff - Bert Pittaway, Neil Woledge; from Yoho - Jim Sime, Johnny Romonson; and from Jasper - Tom Ross, Murray Dawson and myself.

During the six weeks we were on course, we skied every potential ski area in Jasper, Banff and Yoho under every possible winter condition. Noel, (known as Snowflake to his students), was an aggressive instructor with no let up in the pace he set from the first day. Our training grounds included Maligne Lake, Marmot Basin, Columbia Icefield, Mt. Norquay, Lake Louise, Mt. Whitehorn and the little Yoho valley. We stayed in work camps or alpine huts, many of them without the basic amenities but located close to the areas we skied so no time was lost in unnecessary travel.

We soon realized how poorly we were equipped for a training course of this kind. Our outer clothing was too heavy or too light. Our skis were not designed for deep snow skiing. The bindings were a combination of downhill and touring and inappropriate for either mode of travel. The climbing skins were army surplus and we usually didn't have the right type of ski wax for the snow conditions.

We survived the course and came home wiser in the ways of ski mountaineering. There were no serious accidents except one that came close to injuring our instructor. Noel was demonstrating the technique of arresting a fall if your partner on your rope fell into a crevasse. To add realism to the exercise, he tied himself on to the rope and showed the other skier how to hold him if he fell. Then he deliberately jumped over a cornice to simulate a fall. What he didn't do was check the height of the cornice and he landed on the snowpack below before the rope became taut. We all looked in disbelief over the edge to see Noel lying in the snow with the wind knocked out of him. The impulse was to laugh but we were not sure if we had a real rescue to perform. Soon Noel was on his feet admitting that it was a pretty stupid manoeuvre.

Johnny Romonson added some diversity to the program.

Many days we made a ski ascent to the summit of a mountain. By the time we reached the top, some of us were exhausted and not looking forward to a deep-snow ski descent. Johnny's solution was to unfurl a war surplus cargo parachute and tie the shrouds around his waist. Pointing his skis straight down the mountain, he pushed off and before he had attained an out-of-control speed, the chute opened and he descended ever so gracefully, most of the time.

We had time before the spring thaw to practise our ski mountaineering skills in the Marmot Basin. Some of the more venturesome deep snow skiers were tracking the various possible ski runs and testing their skill when the inevitable happened.

Charlie Dupre, a recent immigrant to Canada, and a strong skier, cut across a steep bowl and was buried in an avalanche. This first fatality was recorded and the Park Service ski-mountaineering search and rescue duties became apparent.

No sooner had I returned to the district when Chief Warden Brodie phoned to ask if I wanted to transfer to the Sunwapta district with the headquarters on the highway at Poboktan Creek. For six years I had waited for such an opportunity and in the best interests of my family, accepted.

It had taken us a year of hard work to make the Jacques Lake cabin a comfortable home. I had worked long hours packing in every convenience and comfort we needed expecting to stay for a few years and now it was time to move again. Elated with the thought of the cabin on the highway and depressed with the thought of moving out I started packing. Only our most prized possessions, including the sewing machine came out and we left the rest of the furniture for the next occupant.

Sunwapta District – Poboktan Creek, 1957. Note baby Tom hanging on the sign post.

Summers on a highway district are hectic and the summer of 1953 had some added problems. The road from Poboktan Creek to the Columbia Icefield was under construction and heavy rains had the road bed almost impassable. Jasper was hosting a movie production company filming the story, "River Of No Return." The stars were Marilyn Monroe and Robert Mitchum and many of the scenes were shot in the Columbia Icefields area. Long delays waiting for road construction equipment to clear the road made camera crews very impatient, especially when the sun was making infrequent appearances. On one occasion a fuel truck caught fire and the driver, with clothes flaming, panicked and ran into the bush above the road and disappeared. When I requested help from the film crew to search for the driver everyone responded willingly. Driving cattle over the Icefields was part of the show and an unplanned ice fall almost destroyed the cattle herd. Another film crew working at the Columbia Icefields but arriving from the Banff side were producing the story "Saskatchewan." Shelly Winters and Alan Ladd were the stars. The story included Mounties trying to prevent Indian uprisings.

Very few days passed without incidents that required a Park Warden's emergency response in the Columbia Icefields area. Easy access to the glaciers encouraged the most inexperienced visitor to get into trouble. With the proper training and adequate equipment, Park Wardens soon became well-qualified to execute difficult rescues successfully.

13

JOHN McGILLVRAY
AN UNSOLVED MYSTERY

O N Sunday, June 28, a man had walked into the yard at the Athabasca Falls warden station early in the morning and asked my Dad for a bar of soap and a towel so he could go to the spring and have a wash. When he returned the soap and towel, Dad asked him if he'd like to have breakfast. He replied that it didn't hurt him to go without food for two weeks at a time and still be able to walk 30 miles a day. As he left the station, Dad asked his name and he said he was John McGillivray. Further questioning revealed he had come from Ontario to the Edson area seeking work in the bush without success and was still searching.

Leaving the warden station, McGillivray continued south on the highway. After thinking over his discussion with McGillivray and deciding his behaviour unusual, Dad contacted the R.C.M.P. Corporal Duff from the Jasper detachment came out and located McGillivray 15 miles further south and stopped him for questioning. Unable to establish any reason to detain him he let him go.

As the summer passed, no further thought was given to this incident. I made a patrol to the Waterfalls cabin in mid-July and noticed that someone had been in the cabin and had taken a small amount of food. Warden Larry McGuire was at Maligne Lake and I phoned him asking if he had registered any hiker out for this area. He said no, so I contacted Norm Hooper's replacement on the Brazeau, a new warden, Fred Comeau. Fred gave the same reply, so I passed it off without further thought and returned to the highway.

Edie and I were expecting our second baby in the early part of August. On August 9th, signs of an impending birth warned us to drive the forty-five miles to town, where she was hospitalized.

Four Point cabin – Final resting place of John McGillvray, 1953.

Leaving Debbie with Grandma at Athabasca Falls, I went back to Poboktan and on the morning of August 12th received a call from the hospital to tell me the baby was expected soon.

Suzanne Marie was born that night and Edie and baby were doing fine. After visiting Edie and the baby for two days I went back to the district.

Late afternoon on August 18th Warden Fred Comeau had returned to Camp Parker after leaving there in the morning enroute to the Brazeau headquarters over Nigel Pass. He had been in town for a week and on his return had not brought any supplies with him intending to overnight at the Four Point cabin. Arriving at Four Point, signs around the cabin indicated someone had been there recently. The shutters were off the windows and a collection of pots and pans were out front.

When he entered the cabin, he was surprised to find a man lying on the bunk obviously starving. The man was incoherent and unable to communicate except to point feebly to indicate his hunger and emit guttural sounds. There was absolutely no food left in the cabin, and Fred, who had been expecting to use the supplies, had started out without so much as a chocolate bar. Unable to feed the man or himself, he decided to return to Camp Parker for help.

There was no communication outlet at Camp Parker, just a corral and small shed for saddlery and oats, so he hitched a ride to the Columbia Icefields chalet and phoned me at Poboktan cabin. He suggested I come to Camp Parker with a saddle horse in my truck and bring a selection of food to feed the man at Four Point.

I reported to headquarters in Jasper the plan of action and left to join Fred. The time by now was nine o'clock and getting dark. Nigel Pass traverses a rock slide and crossing in the dark was hazardous but the horses had been over this trail often enough to know where they were going.

We arrived at Four Point at midnight and found the person still alive. The air in the cabin was fouled by the victim not having strength enough to properly take care of himself. We lit a candle, started a fire and removed a window so we could stand the smell. Our concern was to try and keep him relaxed while we cooked some chicken noodle soup. Although he couldn't talk properly, his eyes expressed his joy in having someone find him and coming to his rescue.

Above him was a wire line across the room that is used for hanging bedding when away from the cabin. From that he had suspended a set of horse hobbles which he had used to lift himself up and out of the bunk. In bed beside him was a broom, which we interpreted from his actions, was used to chase the ground squirrels away. The turtle-neck sweater he wore appeared far too large for him because of the loss of body weight. The skin on his face was pulled tight and appeared white and waxen. His eyes were huge and glassy, especially in the dim cabin light.

We found some identification on the table that told us his name was John McGillivray but nothing else to help us determine his background.

The soup was soon ready and we knew that he should be given only a few sips of broth at a time as his system was so deteriorated. The eagerness seen in his eyes expressed how anxious he was to be fed. Because of his weak condition I reached behind his head to lift him so he could swallow and Fred held a spoonful of soup ready to feed him.

As I lifted his head I had the feeling that McGillivray had died in the past few moments, with his eyes open and a smile on his face. It was incredible to have this happen when he was so close to being helped. The excitement may have been too much or he had willed himself to live until he would be found. Fred's reaction to this sad event was, "Well, if you don't like my cooking, I'll eat it myself." He sat on the bunk beside John and finished the soup.

With McGillivray's expression unchanged and his eyes wide open we pulled a blanket over him and went outside. Using spare bedding from the cabin we lay under a tree and slept until daylight. With a last look around, we put together the events that must have transpired since McGillivray was seen on the highway June 28, fifty-one days before last night.

After the R.C.M.P. had checked McGillivray just south of Sunwapta Falls he had continued on the highway until he found the trail near the Poboktan cabin that went up Poboktan Creek. He followed the trail to the Waterfalls cabin, broke in and must have stayed for a few days. Continuing on up to the foot of Poboktan Pass, he left the main trail and climbed over Jonas Shoulder at an elevation of 8200 feet, then through Jonas Pass out to Four Point. He must have stayed at Four Point until all the food was gone and then decided to go down the south fork of the Brazeau. When he reached the river crossing at the Brazeau headquarters he was afraid to cross, so he built a wickie-up in the trees near the trail, probably hoping someone would show up at the cabin. When no one came he returned to the Four Point cabin.

Fred had been patrolling near the Isaac Creek area and when he returned to his headquarters he left right away to go to Jasper for a week in town. As he crossed the river he noticed the wickie-up but had given it only a casual glance and continued on up the river. The Four Point cabin is situated on a knoll above the main trail with an access trail leading up to the cabin. Fred stayed on the main trail on his way to Camp Parker, unaware of McGillivray's presence in the cabin.

During the last days of McGillivray's life he must have been too weak to move away from the cabin. The pots and pans outside were used to catch rain dripping from the cabin roof. There was also evidence he ate leaves from the small shrubs growing near the door, which were not properly digested, judging from the smell in the cabin. He had left his boots outside and at some time in his travels had cut the toes out.

In the seven weeks since he was last seen on the highway he had walked at least 60 miles. The only food eaten was a little at Waterfalls cabin and the supplies at Four Point which might have lasted him two or three weeks.

There are a number of "ifs" in this sequence of events. If McGillivray had stayed on the main trail from Waterfalls cabin he would have easily reached Poboktan shelter and if he continued on, would have arrived at the Brazeau headquarters. Instead he chose to climb Jonas Shoulder and came out at Four Point. If he had followed the trail from Four Point in the opposite direction going upstream, he would have reached the highway in one day. If when he did come out at the Brazeau cabin and waded the river he would have found all the food he needed. If Fred had returned while McGillivray was camped at the Brazeau crossing, he could have helped him. If Fred had stopped at Four Point on his way out the previous week McGillivray may have recovered from his starved condition. But all these "ifs" didn't take place and John McGillivray lay dead in the cabin.

We returned to the highway that morning and contacted the R.C.M.P. Constable Kelsburgh came out and returned to the cabin with Fred to investigate. They rolled him in some roofing material and buried him behind the cabin near a large rock. A follow-up by the R.C.M.P. resulted in their finding a brother in the maritimes and advised him of his death.

14

THE ANNUAL FALL BOUNDARY PATROLS TO MONITOR HUNTING AND TRAPPING ACTIVITIES

W ITH the McGillivray incident concluded it was time to prepare for a patrol along the southern section of the Park boundary. I found time to visit Edie and Suzanne in the hospital and when the time came, brought them home, as well as Deborah from her Grandma's. A week later I left for a game patrol to the Brazeau district.

Fred Comeau decided to leave the warden service soon after the McGillvray case and his horses had to be trucked from Camp Parker to Poboktan cabin. In preparation for the boundary game patrol, it was necessary to have his horses re-shod. I went to town to pick up the blacksmith and return to Poboktan cabin.

Passing the Sunwapta Bungalow resort I saw a car had stopped on the driving lane and the driver was feeding a bear through the car window. I pulled ahead of the bear and car stopping about 200 feet beyond. I commented to the blacksmith that people in their excitement to see and feed a bear, often overlook their safety and the safety of other travellers. With this on my mind, I walked back to the car approaching on the opposite side from the bear. The passenger rolled the window down and I repeated the same message, but received an indifferent response. To make a greater impression I suggested if they continued feeding the bear they would be charged under the National Parks regulations.

This time the response was instant and the car drove away. This left me standing nose to nose with a bear expecting to be given another cookie. Knowing the consequences for not having a cookie, I headed for the truck running as fast as I could. My patrol truck was a vintage Ford with running boards and by the time I reached the truck, with the bear in hot pursuit, I dared not back up to open the door.

Jumping on the running board I called to the blacksmith through the open window to pass me my rifle that I carried behind the seat. In the meantime the bear had grabbed my heel and was trying to pull me from the truck. The rifle was passed to me but I could not use both hands to put a cartridge in the chamber. To gain a little time, I hit the bear on the nose with the rifle barrel and he let go of my foot.

I had a moment before he recovered to load the rifle and as he looked up at me I fired, killing him. So much for the poor bear. If the park visitors would only realize the problems they create by feeding wild animals. Often this thoughtless act signs the bear's death warrant when it becomes aggressive and injures someone.

Fred Comeau's replacement was Bud Binning, who would be staying on the Brazeau district for the winter. Wardens Murray Dawson and Armand Hanley came out from town and the four of us travelled to Isaac Creek where we would be patrolling from for the next three weeks.

During this time of the year, there were always hunting parties moving up and down the Brazeau River across from the Park. Job Creek was a favourite point of access and a good area for sheep and goat. The Bighorn Trail was another well-travelled route through the Park between the Dowling Ford and the Southesk River.

Frank Wells, after retiring from the Warden Service, had a big game guiding and outfitting business and hunted the Brazeau River valley. His semi-permanent camp was located on the east side of the river seven miles down stream from the Brazeau cabin.

One misfortune that Frank had while hunting was having a hunter die of a heart attack. The hunter was an elderly person and a little overweight. The weather was warm and soon after death, the corpse began to expand from gas. Frank couldn't get it to drape over a pack saddle so he made a small incision with his pocket knife to relieve the pressure and was able to pack the body to the highway.

Directly across from the Wells camp on a high hill near the river and in the Park was an Indian unnamed grave with an enclosure and marked with a cross. I never could find out who was buried there. Mrs. Suzette Swift, wife of Louis Swift, was a frequent visitor to our home in Jasper and one day I asked her if she recalled anything about the grave site on the Brazeau. She didn't, but insisted she knew of a trading post at Brazeau Lake. At the time of our discussion, Mrs. Swift was a very old lady and I thought she may have the location confused with some other trading post she may have visited as a young woman. Her state-

Jim Simpson's trapper cabin one mile downstream from Brazeau Lake.

ment often came to mind when I was at the lake but I found no evidence of any buildings.

There was an old trapper cabin between the lake and Brazeau cabin that I thought had been one of old Jim Simpson's. Years later in 1968 when working in Banff I had occasion to meet with Mr. Simpson at his home and I asked if he recalled the cabin on the Brazeau. He told me it was one of his. He also alluded to the good sheep range on the slopes above the cabin where exceptional trophy head sheep were shot and the capes and horns packed back to Banff to be sold.

The game patrol passed without any special incident and we returned to the highway in mid-September. At home Edie was recovering from a scare she had a couple of days before my return. Hearing someone at the back door she went to see who was there and was surprised by a bear trying to come in. I had left her with instructions on how to handle a .455 Smith & Wesson revolver that made a terrific noise when discharged and packed a heavy load of lead for a short distance.

When she returned to the door with the revolver, the bear had stepped off the porch and was swiping at the basement windows trying to break the glass. There were a number of windows on the main floor that hinged opening inwards. Standing at the open window above the bear she opened fire to scare him away. The bear backed away from one basement window and started circling the cabin. Edie ran downstairs to close the window she knew was open where the firewood was thrown in, and came back upstairs following the bear's movements, blasting away whenever she saw him.

He finally left, leaving her badly shaken, imagining herself and her two small children in a cabin with a cantankerous bear. She took me to the basement and showed me all the muddy bear paw prints on the outside of the window panes. The question was why had the bear been so persistent? Had he been successful in entering other buildings and obtaining food?

Between late fall and early winter, in extremely cold weather, the lakes and streams freeze over before the heavy snows fall. This is the best time to travel on foot to the more inaccessible areas of the mountains. Crossing frozen swamps, beaver dams, lakes or rivers enables a person to take the most direct route to his destination.

These were the conditions in November 1953 when I received a phone call from Charlie Blackman, living at Tete Jaune Cache. Charlie had taken the Fortress Lake trapline back after Louis Reese had quit and he asked me if I would like to travel with him for a few days.

There is a real advantage, when you have an opportunity to visit a new area with someone who has already been there, to take the time to go. Casual discussions provide information on game movements, good fishing waters, local names of various features, trail locations and past human activities that all add up to a more personal knowledge of the area. We set a date of November first to meet at Sunwapta Falls.

Soon after crossing the Sunwapta River over a narrow bridge, we were in the Athabasca valley following the river until the Chaba River forks and up the Chaba River to Fortress Lake, a distance of thirteen miles. The trip that day was cold but good travelling. The park boundary at the east end of the lake is also the inter-provincial boundary and is defined by the height of land and watershed.

At the boundary there is a cluster of three cabins. One on the Park side built years ago by Warden Frank Wells, another on a bench overlooking the lake that was abandoned, and in between, Charlie's trapper cabin. The trapper cabin was well constructed with whip-sawn lumber for the roof, door, furniture and floor. This cabin was more elaborate than most trapper cabins. I commented on the well-built features and Charlie told me the lumber had been taken from the warden cabin apparently without the Park's consent or concern.

A short distance from the cabin was an open spring near an A-frame shelter that sometime in the past was used for winter boat storage. In the open spring water was a school of fish all about two pound size that wouldn't take a baited hook. Charlie and I went back to the cabin to make a dip net from the window screen. Returning to the spring we selectively caught the fish we needed for ourselves and for Charlie to prepare trap bait for his trap sets.

The next time I saw Frank Wells, I asked about the warden cabin at Fortress Lake. During construction Frank was chopping out the logs for the window frame. Twisting about to chop the top log level, he hurt his back. From the conversation I understood the construction came to an end and the cabin was never finished. This may be the reason the Park showed no interest when building materials were taken for the trapper's cabin.

When Charlie was ready to set his traps I returned to the highway. The snowshoeing was good with only enough snow to cover the rocks on the miles of gravel bar the winter trail followed. When I reached the river crossing on the Athabasca the wind had blown the river ice clear of snow. I picked a section of the river where the water ran slowly and the ice looked safe. I started across with my snowshoes on to spread my body weight and lessen the chance of falling through.

About half way across, the downstream snowshoe broke through the ice. Fortunately the ice held me but the current in the river pulled at my snowshoe, making it difficult to bring it back though the hole in the ice. Afraid to move about too much in case I broke through completely, I patiently kept trying to get my snowshoe free. After a few anxious minutes I was free and got to shore. I changed my socks and continued to the highway and home.

15

1954 – THE YEAR OF MANY ACHIEVEMENTS. NEW BUILDINGS, MORE TRAINING, HOME IMPROVEMENTS

I N early January 1954 after a Christmas break, Warden Bud Binning and I left for Poboktan Pass with a plan for Bud to continue on to Brazeau cabin and I would return to Poboktan cabin. The temperature was holding between 35 below and 40 below F. We stopped at the Waterfalls cabin overnight and left for the pass the next morning. Coming out of the timber into the high country we faced a strong cold east wind. By the time we reached the foot of the pass we were in a whiteout with blizzard conditions and unable to find our way and had to return to Waterfalls. The next morning the wind was down but still cold. We made it into the pass and Bud went on to Brazeau and I returned to Poboktan.

The cold weather continued and lakes were freezing to a depth of over two feet. This had the advantage of allowing the project of building a new warden's cabin on the far shore of Maligne Lake. The road was ploughed from Jasper along the shore of Medicine Lake, then followed the old tote road to Maligne Lake and across the ice to the new cabin site. Many of the old Ford patrol trucks had been replaced with the four wheel drive Willys half tons. Six of these trucks travelled in convoy hauling building materials and supplies for the station.

Truck convoy crossing Maligne Lake on the return trip to Jasper after unloading building materials for cabin.

During the haul, Dad, one of the regular drivers, became ill and I had the opportunity to participate. At the time I thought this was real progress compared to my previous experience in cabin building when everything had to be transported by pack horse. It was the first time a water well was dug below the cabin foundation to supply a water pressure system.

In March Noel Guardener returned to Jasper to hold a local ski-mountaineering school for the Jasper wardens. The school was less of a test of endurance than the previous school and a greater emphasis placed on proper equipment and technical downhill deep snow skiing. The basics were demonstrated and applied on the Whistler Ski Hill, then we moved on to Marmot Basin. Terrain analysis gave everyone an appreciation of the importance of route selection for a ski ascent of a mountain and the importance of avoiding exposure to avalanche dangers. Explosives were carried to the upper slopes of the mountain and after a demonstration on analyzing snow stability, explosions were detonated to release avalanches. Time was spent in the Bald Hills above Maligne Lake and the last trip was to the Tonquin valley and the alpine hut at Outpost Lake.

At the same time a group of skiers from Edmonton were planning an expedition to travel from Jasper to Banff following as close as possible along the Great Divide. If my memory is correct the two promoters and organizers of the adventure were Pat Boswell and Lloyd Tyrell. There were grave doubts and misgivings by the Park wardens that the members of this expedition had sufficient knowledge or qualifications to undertake such an ambitious trip. The route selected was exposed to rough terrain and avalanche hazards. General weather conditions had been poor all spring. I was not aware of any briefing given to the Park Service on details of the expedition. Certainly nothing was passed on to the wardens who were located along the proposed route who were expected to intercept the skiers as they moved south to check on their progress.

In preparation for the trip, air drops of supplies were made at points the skiers hoped to reach. The only cache I was aware of was dropped on Fortress Lake. The supplies were packaged in plywood boxes about 18 inches square with a long pole and flag attached. By early April the expedition was still in the Jasper area and had abandoned the idea. On April 6, Tom McCready and John Dupre, the brother of Charlie Dupre who had died the previous year in an avalanche in Marmot Basin, came from Jasper with a Bombardier snowmobile to Sunwapta Falls. I met them and we went to Fortress Lake and recovered the food cache.

Spring skiing in Marmot Basin was excellent and becoming

ever more popular with both local and Edmonton skiers. I was kept on as a ski patrolman in Marmot until the Warden's Spring Training School started at the end of April. The syllabus of a spring school varied little from year to year. Fire suppression was top priority and everyone had the opportunity to operated fire pumps and lay out fire lines. The R.C.M.P. briefed us on law enforcement procedures and Bill Cleveland gave a session on telephone maintenance. Basic first aid was discussed and a doctor showed X-rays of different fractures and the importance of properly handling a victim. Mouth to mouth resuscitation and cardiopulmonary resuscitation had yet to be developed as first-aid treatment.

A rabies outbreak in the province alerted dog and cat owners to have their pets protected. The Park provided the vaccine and Warden Jack McGee was the administrator. Many of the town dogs and cats ran about out of control and without a licence until the inoculation program started. A licence was required before the inoculation would be given. The wardens now had an opportunity to record the animal's owner.

Warden Bud Binning, after spending a winter on the Brazeau requested a transfer to town and exchanged positions with Warden Armand Hanley. I went with Warden Hanley to the Brazeau to help him get organized and familiar with the area. While there I found my own horses, Peanuts, Popcorn and Black Hawk and brought them back to Poboktan. They had wintered well. Popcorn was old enough to work so was sold to an outfitter for ten dollars.

We were expecting our third child in the fall and with the extra work for Edie in raising a family with primitive utilities and facilities, I started a project to improve conditions. With a 45 gallon gas drum in the basement hooked up to a coil of pipes in the wood heater and then filling the drum with buckets of water from the creek we had hot water. The water circulating through this system combined with frequent air locks produced the most unusual sound. Everytime it burped you expected it to explode.

An old electric washing machine was converted by using a small air-cooled gas driven engine called an "Iron Horse." Without adequate tools to do a proper job the Iron Horse and washing machine were bolted on a wooden platform close together and connected with a drive belt between the two pulleys.

The first load of washing was prepared and with a firm push on a lever to start the motor, we were in the laundry business. The difference in the pulley ratio between the electric motor and the gas motor with the larger pulley, operated the machine at triple the normal speed. It took both of us to keep the whole unit from walking across the basement floor because of the vibration. Once the dolly inside the tub began gyrating, the soap suds foamed out. We shortened the wash cycle to about half the time because of the increased speed and then proceeded to wringing out the clothes. When the wringer engaged, the rollers literally spun and each article had to be fed through very carefully. As soon as the wringer grabbed a diaper, it passed through and shot out like someone dealing a deck of cards, or else wound around a roller in record time almost destroying the material. Amid gales of laughter we got the job done in record time. To top off the story, the name of our washing machine was "Locomotive," which we had bought secondhand just before getting married.

With the washing more or less resolved, I dug a ditch from the creek to the cabin and ran a pipe into the basement and the water would almost make it to the cabin by gravity. With the help of a circular action gas barrel pump hooked up to a stationary bicycle and connected to the water intake, we had running water in the basement. The volume of water used was regulated by the time you spent pedalling the bicycle. The next step was to get cold water into the kitchen.

Three gas barrels were hauled into the attic and hooked in tandem. A pipe from the basement pump filled the tank and another pipe, from the barrels to the kitchen brought water to the kitchen sink. Occupants before us must have dreamed of having water someday because the pantry had been converted to a bathroom with a toilet bowl and

Saturday night bath – Diane and John.

bathtub draining into a septic tank outside. Water was not hooked up before our time though the cabin was built in 1939.

By hooking up these two conveniences we were very comfortable. Hot water had to be carried from the basement but that was not bad considering what we had before. Guests found it very entertaining when they wanted to use the toilet and flush it—they first had to go pedal the bike in the basement.

Electric lights came next when I bought a 500 watt portable generator from a construction company. The number of bulbs we had was limited to the power wattage but still better than lanterns. To further add to the comfort of the cabin I built a small brick fireplace with a propane heater insert. We were very thankful for this feature when we would return to a cold cabin after being in town and be able to light this source of heat instantly before our wood heater in the basement could warm the cabin.

The next spring the government decided to institute a rental charge on all warden station accommodation based on a number of factors including isolation, size of building, age of building and of all things, the conveniences of lights, heat and water that I had installed myself at my own expense. With take-home pay of less than $50.00 a week, any rental charge was a financial blow.

The Brazeau district warden was always at a disadvantage when he stopped at the Poboktan cabin either returning from the district or departing for the Brazeau. Accommodation was a problem when the resident warden had a family and the cabin fully occupied or the two wardens really didn't care for each other's company. To resolve this problem a small two-room cabin was constructed in the yard and both wardens had the option to be independent.

Many of the old ways of a warden's life were slowly changing. Visitor demands were increasing and a warden had less time to do the things he thought should be done. To better utilize his time it was necessary to improve communications. The Parks had a consultant from the Marconi Company making radio signal tests along the road from Banff to Jasper. With repeater stations strategically placed at certain locations along the highway, instant communication was possible by mobile or portable radios.

In the previous year the trail crew had pushed a fire road from Sunwapta Falls to the Athabasca River near the mouth of the Chaba River and this year built a frame shelter cabin at a lake called Long Lake. Clarence Long was the foreman but the lake was also long and narrow so it was never settled how the lake was named. It was possible to drive my patrol truck to the cabin site. The most thrilling part of the trip was to squeeze the truck across the narrow footbridge at Sunwapta Falls and attain enough speed to climb the rock shelf at the far end of the bridge. Edie was reluctant to ride across the bridge with the babies, but once across enjoyed the trip to the cabin. Fishing was good, and the kids enjoyed travelling with Susie in a carriage and Debbie standing in a 5-gallon can strapped to my packboard. We enjoyed a surprise visit from John Dupre and a bottle of fine brandy was memorable.

It was time for the annual game patrol and Hanley and I left on August 20th for the Brazeau River. Wardens Dawson and Binning followed a few days later and we continued on to Isaac Creek.

One morning at daylight we heard the wolves howling on the flats near the cabin and Barney started barking back. A few

A wolf shot while attempting to kill Barney. Wardens Armand Hanley, Bud Binning and Murray Dawson stationed at Isaac Creek cabin during the hunting season border patrol.

moments later we heard a fight outside and when I checked, Barney and a wolf were in serious combat. Bud had followed me outside bringing his rifle with him and as soon as he had a clear shot he killed the wolf.

Each year that I patrolled the Brazeau district I tried to explore some remote area where I had never previously patrolled. This year my plan was to travel up Isaac Creek from the cabin about nine miles to a small lake. From the lake there is a small stream coming from the west that I intended to follow to a summit at about the 8500 foot level and then descend into the headwaters of the south branch of the Southesk River. Warden Hanley agreed to come with me and on the morning of September 14th we left Isaac Creek. There was a good trail high on the south bank of Isaac Creek which we followed until it crossed the creek and continued on over the Don Hoover trail.

We continued following Isaac Creek through open buck-brush flats until we reached the small lake and then swung west climbing steadily. Nearing the summit we had to climb a steep talus slope of loose moving rock. The horses had difficulty keeping their footing. Frequent rests were necessary so they wouldn't play out and refuse to climb. When we reached the summit the view was spectacular. The whole Southesk valley lay below us but the drop-off directly ahead was so steep we couldn't see if we could get down.

(Above) On the summit between the headwaters of Isaac Creek and Southesk River. This is the first known recorded crossing.
(Below) Descending into the Southesk drainage. Note the faint line of horse tracks crossing the talus slope.

After the horses had rested we started down hoping we would get a look at what was below and if it was passable. We certainly didn't want to have to climb back up and backtrack the way we had come. Most of the mountain was talus rock that moved as we traversed on an angle towards the head of the basin. By now I could see we couldn't go straight down because of a band of rock crossing the face of the mountain. Staying a distance above the rock cliff to minimize the danger of getting carried down in the moving talus I kept angling towards the head of the basin. The rock finally petered out and we made it to the valley floor with some difficulty.

Exhausted, we camped in the first open meadow we came to and had a good rest. That evening I thought it appropriate to register our crossing, wondering if we had been the first to come this way with three pack horses, one dog and two saddle horses. I started chopping out a registration plaque on a large spruce tree and the next morning wrote the following inscription: "J.N.P. Game patrol - Warden Frank Camp and Warden Armand Hanley - From Isaac Creek over top of mountain and down creek across valley from this campsite. Hard going all the way from Isaac Creek. Elevation on summit crossed 8500 feet. 5 horses and 1 dog, Barney. Sept. 15, 1954." The words of this inscription were transcribed from an old photograph I took at the site.

The next morning we continued down the south fork of the Southesk River and I soon recognized some familiar landmarks from the trip taken earlier with Dr. Flook over the Indian Pass. The next day we camped at Southesk Lake and laid over a day to hike into a small unnamed lake three and a half mile directly south of the lower end of Southesk Lake. Grizzly signs were everywhere.

On our way to the Poboktan cabin after the game patrol, Warden Hanley and I discussed the idea of building an emergency shelter at the Jonas Trail cutoff below Poboktan Pass. By the time we reached the highway we had a plan to go ahead and construct a small cabin on the hillside in the forks of the trail.

Packs of building materials were assembled including tools, a stove and cooking utensils, and packed back to the building site. To prepare a level site we dug back into the hillside until the cut bank was about three feet high. Timber was scarce but thirty trees were selected, felled and skidded to the site. For the side walls of the cabin we placed all the butts to the front end. The butts of the logs for the front and back walls were alternated. With this design the flat roof had an adequate slope to the back. Over a couple of rafters we nailed on a lumber roof. A small step-over door was cut out and a bunk built across the back of the cabin. An airtight heater was added. All this in four days and we had a shelter where only a few years before Edie, Dad and I sat under a tree in the dead of winter beside a fire waiting for daylight. The final touch was to run a line from the main telephone line to the cabin and connect the telephone.

In the late fall, I occupied my time with work that kept me close to Poboktan Creek. Our third baby was expected in early November and I wanted to be sure when the time came I

Warden Hanley in the doorway of our newly constructed shelter at the forks of the Jonas trail and Poboktan Pass, 1954.

wouldn't be too far away. We took the two girls to visit with their grandmother in Edmonton for the first week of October. It was also the time of year that wardens organized a schedule for wood cutting with a buzz saw. Once each warden had stock-piled his yearly supply of logs for firewood at his highway cabin they helped each other cutting wood. Portable chain saws had yet to be introduced to the district wardens.

November 3rd, 1954 was the day we had been waiting for and we made the early morning 45 mile trip to the hospital in time for Edie to give birth to a baby girl later that day. The next morning when the nurse brought baby Diane Marie to Edie for nursing they had her long, thick, black hair tied up in a blue ribbon. I took the rest of my holidays to babysit Debbie and Suzie until Edie returned home with Diane.

On December 4th I received word that Warden Bob Jones was missing. Bob, a confirmed bachelor, had for years been the district warden at Blue Creek. When Warden Frank Burstrom transferred to the town-site from Devona, Bob moved to the Miette district. Long before becoming a warden, Bob had worked as a packer and trail hand for many of the local outfitters.

After years of living alone he had become very independent and I recall he wouldn't even take the advantage of following another warden's snowshoe trail up the Snake Indian River enroute to his home at Blue Creek. Frank Burstrom told me that when they travelled together to Willow Creek their snowshoe tracks would be parallel to one another. At the Shale Banks cabin where they would stop overnight, Bob would insist on having his own salt and pepper shakers on the table.

After moving to Devona, Bob Jones's social life when in town centred about the Astoria Hotel where he enjoyed the company of many of his old friends. After he left Jasper on December 4th, 1954 to go back to Devona, he failed to report in the following morning. A check was made at his cabin and signs indicated he had arrived home but he was not around. The waterpail was missing and the assumption was he had gone to the river for water.

The Snake Indian River that flows past the back of the cabin freezes over in winter and Bob had a hole cut through the ice where he dipped the waterpail. It was likely when Bob went to fill the pail, the current caught the pail catching him off balance pulling him headlong under the ice. On April 15, 1955 after the ice had started to break up, Bob's body was found on a gravel bar near the railroad crossing of the river about half a mile away. He was buried in Jasper on April 18th.

One of Bob's prized possessions was a coffee cup that sat on the window sill above the wash basin. During the filming of the "River Of No Return," the company was shooting near the cabin and Bob invited Marilyn Monroe in for coffee. She accepted, and when drinking the coffee, left a lipstick imprint of her lips on the edge of the cup. Bob placed it on the window sill unwashed and from then on it was look but don't touch.

CHAPTER

16

1955 – WARDEN HANLEY BURIED IN A SNOWSLIDE. THE SKULL OF MISSING TOWERMAN FOUND. ROCK CLIMBING SCHOOLS.

THE first patrol in the new year 1955 was with Charlie Blackman to Fortress Lake. The next trip was to the Brazeau with Warden Hanley. On my return I went to town to pick up my new four wheel drive Willys patrol vehicle. The expectations I had when I began driving this new truck far exceeded its capabilities. I found I was stuck more often with four wheel drive power than with the old Ford. At least I knew the Ford couldn't make it so I'd back off.

Armand Hanley had made a patrol of the Brazeau district and came to town for a few days. On his way back to the district I gave him Barney to pack some of the supplies he had bought from town. He checked in with me the first night at Waterfalls cabin. The next night he called from Poboktan shelter and Edie answered. She could hardly understand what he was saying. He sounded scared and excited and after speaking with him for a few minutes she asked me to take the phone. He told me he had crossed Poboktan Pass without any problem but as he dropped into the stream bed that flows from the pass he was caught in a snowslide.

The slide had started when his weight settled the snowpack and a cornice from the north side about fifty feet above him, broke away and buried him. Completely buried he knew he was in the upright position because the parka hood fell over his forehead when he pushed the snow from his face with his left hand. He had been leading Barney because Barney had been reluctant to leave me at Poboktan cabin. With the leash around his right wrist, it had twisted his right arm behind him. Pushing with his left hand in the direction of the surface he could see daylight through a thin layer of snow. Using his sunglasses in the tips of his fingers, he extended his reach and by making a circular motion he cleared the snow above him.

He started to dig himself out by taking a handful of snow and throwing it out of the hole above. Often the snow was too dry to pack and he had to blow on it in his hand to make it form a ball. Digging down to one knee he was able to pull one foot free from the snowshoe harness and bracing himself pulled the other foot free. The effort to free his feet from the snowshoes had pulled the muscles in his legs and ankles and caused severe pain. When he eventually worked his way to the surface he helped Barney out, who was being held down by his pack under the snow. Without trying to recover his snowshoes he started for Poboktan shelter about a mile away. To assist himself to travel over the snow, he chopped off two large spruce branches that he would lay out in front of him and crawl over. Once he was down in the creek he was then able to wade through the snow.

From his conversation it sounded as though he wasn't in too bad shape except for pulled muscles and would call me again as soon as he had a rest. I phoned headquarters and reported the accident. I asked if someone could come out from town with an extra pair of snowshoes and accompany me over the Pass to Warden Hanley. When Armand phoned again he sounded better and I told him what we'd do.

The next day Murray Dawson came out and the following morning we left Poboktan cabin early. Travelling was good on the packed snowshoe trail and by noon we were at Waterfalls. Our next stop was the shelter at Jonas and after having tea, thought we could make it over the pass before dark. As we passed the avalanche site we could see first-hand how Armand had freed himself from the slide. The hole that he crawled out of was still open and snowballs were laying about. We arrived at Poboktan cabin to find Armand in good spirits and moving about without too much discomfort. This was the first trip that I had ever made from Poboktan cabin to Poboktan shelter in one day on snowshoes, a distance of about 20 miles. We laid over for a day of rest and returned with Barney to the highway in one day leaving Armand to carry on to Brazeau.

Another ski-mountaineering school was organized and the instructor was a famous mountain guide, Hans Moser, originally from Austria. Wardens from Banff and Jasper participated and the training took on a more professional and technical approach.

We camped at the Snowmobile Tours cabins at the Columbia Icefields and trained on the Athabasca Glacier. Part of the training included traversing icefalls on the glacier over snow bridges while roped together, as well as rescue recovery techniques out of crevasses. Although it was the end of March the weather was extremely cold and some wardens were experiencing frost bite. From the Icefields we moved to Marmot Basin for avalanche rescue training including search and probe procedures.

Another shake-up was taking place in the Warden Service. Warden Norman Young would be moving to the Snaring district from the Whirlpool, Armand Hanley to the Whirlpool, and a newcomer from Banff, Mike Schintz would take over the Brazeau. Bud Binning resigned.

Warden Schintz came out to look things over and decided to spend sometime in upgrading the Brazeau stopover cabin in the Poboktan cabin yard. The annual spring fire school had just finished and this was followed by the rock climbing school.

Walter Perren had been appointed Assistant Chief Warden of Banff National Park and assigned the impossible task of training all able bodied wardens in the Western Region on how to be mountain climbers. Walter came from Switzerland and made his first ascent of the Matterhorn at the age of ten. He was the most patient, capable and qualified mountain climbing instructor we could hope to have. In time he developed an elite mountain rescue organization within the Warden Service.

The Jasper rock school was held along the East Highway on the lower slopes of the Colin Range and each climber progressed at his own speed. For some, hanging from a cliff with their fingernails came naturally and for others it was with total fear. If we had been given a choice, most would have gone home. When the school was over, we were still alive, and we returned to our regular work.

What we didn't realize, this was only an introduction to a rock school scheduled for the fall in Banff. We had time between these two schools to keep in touch with what was happening on our districts.

Warden Schintz had moved his horses out from town while he worked on the stopover cabin. His saddle horse got away and disappeared. It was a young horse and not familiar with the country. There were no tracks on any of the trails leading away from the area to suggest he may have pulled out, but search as we did for days we didn't find him. Mike just wouldn't give up and started looking in the most unlikely places. Sure enough high on the wooded sloped on the Endless Chain ridge he was found without adequate food or water and no reason to be there.

We had another welcome visit from John Dupre, with his gift of fresh fruit as before at Jacques Lake and Chaba. The weather was ideal for climbing and we decided to make an ascent of Mt. Athabasca.

We left early the next morning with crampons, ice axe, a rope and a packsack between the two of us for our lunch and camera. We free climbed with no intention of roping up until we made the traverse. We stopped for a rest and I had taken the packsack and continued climbing. After taking no more than a few steps, I broke through the ice and fell until the packsack held me. With John's assistance, I climbed out and looked down into the small hole where I had dropped. The small hole was the apex of a large crevasse and without the packsack I would have fallen through. We roped up immediately and continued to the summit at an elevation of 11,452 feet. The view of the 110 square miles of the Columbia Icefields and surrounding mountains was spectacular.

One night, one of the Chinese cooks at the Columbia Icefield chalet phoned to report a bear in the kitchen and what could they do about it? Edie relayed the message to me and not realizing that I was talking back to her in my sleep, she gave them the message, "Frank said to throw a bucket of hot water at the bear." Edie came back to bed and nothing further was said. When we got up in the morning, Edie was preoccupied with the three little girls and told me the cook hadn't phoned back so everything must have been alright.

I thought I'd better check at the chalet kitchen to show my concern. I was greeted by two exuberant and excited Chinese cooks who couldn't thank me enough for the wonderful advice I had give them. From the conversation, I learned that it was two grizzlies that had come into the kitchen and had started helping themselves to everything they could find. That's when the cook had phoned and talked to Edie.

On the strength of advice that Edie had passed on to them, they were successful in chasing the bears away. As one cook told me, "Hot water good, bear go like hell up mountain." I was thankful the bears did take flight instead of completely destroying the kitchen and maybe doing something worse. later I told Edie, from now on she'd better make sure I was completely awake when there was a message.

With the many transfers of wardens to different districts and preoccupied with their own work only Warden Schintz and I made the game patrol this fall. Mike was anxious to travel over the district and take inventory. He would pack in his winter supplies after the patrol was over. I had left Peanuts and Black Hawk on the Brazeau the previous fall for the winter. Checking with Warden Hanley last spring, he reported them in excellent condition and had come through the winter in great shape. As we travelled down to Isaac Creek I kept listening for the high pitched tinkling sound of Peanuts' bell but heard nothing.

Packing Warden Schintz's winter supplies into the Brazeau District.

On a day I was patrolling the Job Creek Flat, I unexpectedly saw Black Hawk alone and no sign of Peanuts. What ever happened to her I never found out. She had come through the winter and should have been with Black Hawk. It's possible an outfitter needed an extra horse or she could have been killed by wolves or a cougar. Whenever I hear horse bells, I listen for that distinctive ring. I brought Black Hawk back with me and turned him loose with other horses in the Athabasca valley.

On the evening of September 18th, Edie answered the phone. It was the lookout towerman at the Geraldine Tower who wanted to talk. He mentioned he found a skull that day while berry picking. For Edie this was not a casual observation so she asked me to take the phone. When I spoke to him about the skull, he explained it was not uncommon to find old Indian skulls in the north where he had grown up. After our visit was over I kept thinking about the skull and wondered if it had any connection to the disappearance of another lookout tower man in June of 1952.

A new towerman had been hired for the summer of 1952 and because the Geraldine Tower was on the Athabasca district it was Dad's responsibility to take care of the tower site and towerman. Dad picked him up in town with his supplies and with a barrel of water, delivered him to the tower cabin.

A day later he phoned Dad and asked if he could bring up a new stove as the one in the cabin was smoking badly and it wasn't hot enough to cook on. It seemed like a strange request but Dad went to town, picked up a new stove and delivered it to the tower site. Entering the cabin he couldn't believe his eyes. The towerman had been building the fire in the oven! This didn't impress Dad one bit and to add to the problem he was still in bed. He told Dad he was sick and couldn't climb the tower.

Failing to report the next day, Dad went back to the tower and found the cabin locked and the towerman gone. A search party was formed and his footprints were tracked to within two and a half miles from the highway. Random searching for days after failed to turn up any clues to the man's disappearance. Although there was no further evidence of his trail it was expected he had walked to the highway and hitch-hiked out of the park. A new towerman was hired and the mystery was never solved.

Reflecting on this event that took place three years earlier, I wondered if the skull could be that of the lost towerman. Dad was away but expected back the next day and I spoke to him when he returned. He phoned the Chief Warden and asked if a member of the R.C.M.P. would come out and interview the towerman and they went that afternoon. They walked back down the road with the towerman to where he had found the skull and started looking around. Close to where the last tracks were found three years earlier in 1952, they started picking up the bones of a human skeleton scattered over a large area. Nothing was conclusive until a small patch of clothing was found. The cloth was a piece of material from a pair of pants and in the watch pocket was the key to the tower cabin. This was evidence enough to establish the remains as J. Brown, the missing towerman.

The cause of death remains a mystery. When he left the cabin and started down the road he may have been too sick to continue and stepped off the road and died. He may have been lying in the bush when the search party was looking for him and too sick to call for help when they were near. Or he may have been killed by a cougar, as one had been reported seen near the tower earlier. The way the bones were scattered would indicate he had been eaten by some animal.

In October, the advanced school in Banff was held at a camp called Cuthead in the Cascade valley. What we had learned in the spring were the basics on how to climb and now it was time to climb. We roped up in teams of three and always hoped our team-mates were better climbers than yourself. Flints Peak was the favourite training ground and it had something for everyone.

When the exercise to descend with a rescue basket was demonstrated there was a surprising number of volunteers to get in the basket. It was considered safer to let someone lower you down under controlled conditions than to trust your own ability. In the bunkhouse at night, screams of terror were not uncommon as nightmare after nightmare broke the silence.

The grand finale at the end of the school was a simulated rescue. Walter would pick a mountain peak, in this instance, Block Mountain, and taking one of the better climbers with him set up a camp near the mountain top. Then he sent the climber down to report an injured climb-er. The messenger reported to the camp the extent of injury and location of the injured climber. A hasty search and rescue party of seven, me included, left with the minimum amount of required equipment and camping gear and started climbing.

Half way up Block Mountain is a small lake but to reach the lake there is one section of rock that is vertical and must be climbed in a chimney. A fixed rope was secured by the climber who came down to report the accident, but even with this assistance, the climb was unnerving. We reached the lake just before dark and set up camp. The tent of the injured climber was about 2000 feet above us. With three rescue climbers each in two, two-man tents and the seventh climber sleeping in the rescue basket out in the meadow, we slept until daylight.

(Above) A mountain rescue basket exercise. Warden George Wells, an injured climber volunteer, Warden Walter Perren instructing and Warden Jerry Campbell assisting.
(Below) Recovering an injured climber on Block Mountain.

I woke up in a sagging tent, almost suffocating me from the weight of snow that had fallen overnight, and peered outside. Warden Alfie Burstrom was the one sleeping in the rescue basket that was now nothing but a mound of snow on a white landscape. Alfie had a speech impediment and as I watched, this apparition sat upright and with snow falling off him, all he could say was, "Je-Je-Je-Jesus!"

We were soon underway and glad to be climbing to warm up. The rocks were slippery with

new snow. We reached the injured climber (Walter), administered first-aid, and with a victim in the basket started our descent. The exercise was all too real but once back at the camp it felt great to know we could do it if called upon.

There was little time left after the rock school before winter but I wanted to try and reach Fortress Lake with the four wheel drive vehicle. The weather was cold and the river water was low so I thought this would be the time to try. I asked Warden Norm Young if he would like to go with me and we met at Sunwapta Falls.

There was some snow on the trail and when we reached the Athabasca River crossing, ice had started to form on the river banks out to about five feet. The water didn't look too deep to ford, but I knew I couldn't break the ice on the far bank if I tried to cross driving forward. With Norm standing in the back with an axe, I backed out on to the ice which broke away and let us start backing up across the river.

The water was deeper than I had expected but we reached the other side. Norm reached out over the tailgate and chopped a channel. As soon as the back wheels started climbing the bank, the front of the truck angled down and partially went under water, killing the motor. Dead silence as the water in the cab came up over the floor and the only movement was the river flowing by the windshield. A moment of panic when I thought of the jeep frozen in the river for the winter. The only way back the ten miles to the highway would be to wade the river and walk.

An idea came to me which I hoped would work. With the transmission in second gear and releasing the clutch I turned on the key. Slowly the truck started moving across the river with the battery and starting motor providing the power. Once across I tried to start the motor but it wouldn't fire.

First I drained the water and oil out of the crankcase into a pail. When the oil floated to the surface we put it back in the motor. Norm dried the distributor and the motor fired. By now the wheels were frozen and wouldn't turn so we made a torch with a rag and some gas and melted the ice. Soon we were on our way home hardly believing our good luck. Maybe next time we'll make Fortress Lake.

Before now we had been getting by without our own vehicle having the advantage of the Parks liberal policy of letting wardens use the patrol trucks for limited personal use. When the road was closed in the wintertime we would take the family for a drive and Edie would practise her driving skills. Often the road was single-laned with snowbanks on each side and as Edie tried to change gears and steer at the same time, she would hit the snowbanks and a shower of snow would cover the windshield. The kids referred to this as "swimming." After giving us all a few thrills she mastered the skill of driving under adverse conditions and without any great damage to the truck. The cab was getting crowded with three children, three teddy bears, and two adults, especially with one very pregnant mother, so it was time to buy our own vehicle.

Money was our biggest problem but we had saved enough for a down payment and I went to Edmonton and bought a 1952 Plymouth station-wagon. The next problem was to pay off the balance. r took holidays and went to work with a bridge construction company building a new cement bridge over Pobokton Creek right outside our front door.

The job was going well until one cold morning when I was trying to start a Wisconsin gas motor with a hand crank. After numerous attempts to start the motor, it backfired. The crank flew off the end of the crankshaft and hitting my face, cut off a front tooth at the gum level. The exposed nerve in the cold air sent a pain right through me and I ran to the cabin. With tears streaming down my cheeks, I was showing Edie what had happened when Debbie made the unforgettable comment, "I don't cry when my teeth hurt." I drove to Jasper to have the root extracted and it was a couple of days before I went back to work.

The expected date for the arrival of our fourth child was mid-December so on the 14th with the first signs of labour, we went to town and dropped Edie off at the hospital. Returning to the cabin with the three girls, I stopped at Athabasca Falls and asked my mother to come home with us so I would be free to go back to town when I got a telephone call from the hospital. I slept near the phone so I would hear it ring during the night, which it did sometime after midnight. I answered the phone and went back to sleep. In the morning at breakfast my mother asked what the phone call was about during the night. I vaguely remembered answering the phone and then it came back to me in a flash.

Edie had a baby last night, I told her. Once again a question from Mom, "Boy or girl?" When I said I couldn't remember she almost disowned me. I phoned the hospital and mother and baby boy were just fine so I went to town to see our first boy, John Joseph.

After Edie and baby returned home I ski patrolled in the Marmot Basin and Whistler Hill over the Christmas holidays and until mid-January. With better equipment, a new pair of downhill ski boots and greater confidence in my skiing ability, I looked forward to every opportunity to work as a patrolman, while still getting paid for it.

CHAPTER

17

THE ROLE OF THE PARK WARDEN
BECOMES MORE DIVERSE WITH
SEARCH AND RESCUE TOP PRIORITY
AND TRAINING INTENSIFIED

D URING this period of continuous demand for more training to meet the ever increasing need for qualified search
and rescue personnel, I enjoyed good physical health and
was always selected for further training.

My greatest handicap was vertical rock climbing with
absolute terror but somehow I survived. Although the work was
physically demanding it felt good to always be testing myself
against the obstacles the mountains presented. On January 12,
1956 Warden Mike Schintz came out from town on his way to the
Brazeau and I went with him as far as Poboktan Pass. When we
reached the summit the next day we parted company and I came
back. I stayed home for a week and then made a trip into Fortress
Lake returning on the evening of January 22nd.

A message was waiting for me that Mike had failed to report
in and hadn't been heard of since I left him in the Pass. Chief
Warden McGuire directed me to go and look for him. As I was
making preparations to leave for the Brazeau, Mike reported in
that all was well. I don't remember why he had been out of contact but was thankful he was safe.

The spring snow conditions were excellent for skiing. Now
that I was equipped with deep snow skis, good boots and clip-on
skins I started patrolling areas that were normally not visited
when snowshoeing. From the Waterfalls cabin Mike and I
climbed the east shoulder of Waterfalls Peak hoping to cross over
the summit and descend into the Jonas Creek valley and ski out
to the highway and home. The climb was more than we had
expected and we turned back about half way up.

Next I climbed the west shoulder of Wilcox Peak to glass over
a route to the summit of Tangle Ridge which was my next goal.

Mike showed up at Poboktan cabin and I asked him to come along to Tangle Ridge. The day was overcast and cold but after a four hour climb we reached the 9500 foot summit. Soon after we started down a light snow was falling which soon became a whiteout. To ensure we descended along the same ridge we had climbed, we dared not free ski but had to take our time and keep our old tracks in view. Skiing in a whiteout gives the strangest sensation of balance and speed. Your judgement is so distorted you could ski over a cliff as other skiers have done, coming to an untimely death.

Noel Guardener paid us a visit in April and we made a ski ascent over the third icefall on Athabasca Glacier and then on to the 9000 foot level of Snow Dome. Early the next morning before avalanches were likely to start we made another ski ascent to the high col on Mt. Athabasca.

Fred Schleiss, a newcomer to the Park from Austria was hired as a mountaineering search and rescue specialist to be stationed at Columbia Icefields for the summer. For his orientation to the area he stayed at the Poboktan stopover cabin and accompanied me on patrols during May and June. We studied the topographical map of the area and concluded that if we climbed to the summit of Sunwapta Peak at 9897 feet, we would have a good overview of the Columbia Icefields. We also expected to see at least ten mountains over 11,000 feet including Mt. Robson from our vantage point.

On May 28, 1956 the sky was clear and no wind so we made the climb. The view was incredible. Using the book, "The Canadian Alpiner's Guide To The Rockies," a compass, binoculars and topographical map, we checked each mountain as we identified it except Mt. Robson. A haze made it difficult to confirm the Mt. Robson sighting. A view of a massive snowfield where Mt. Robson should be satisfied us that we had Mt. Robson in view.

Fred Schleiss, Park Alpine Specialist on the summit of Mt. Sunwapta.

Near the end of June I was saddened by the news that Warden Frank Bryant had died. Frank had been the town warden when I was growing up in Jasper. As kids, we hunted squirrel and chickens with a variety of weapons in the hills above town.

A high country patrol.

Our greatest fear was to be caught by Warden Bryant because we knew we would have to forfeit our sling shots, bow and arrows or B.B. guns if we got caught. Frank was buried June 30th.

George Bunning and his telephone crew had to be packed to the Jonas cutoff and helped to set up a camp. At long last after years of bandaid maintenance to the telephone line over Poboktan Pass, a completely new pole line was to be constructed from tree line to tree line. Fifty poles would be needed and to find this many suitable trees at timberline was a problem. With selective cutting over a large area on the Waterfalls side of the pass, enough trees were found.

The skid horse could only pull at the most three poles at a time up into the pass. The longest pull was to the far side of the pass, a distance of three miles. They were a hard working crew that did good work and the job was finished in a month.

Dr. Don Flook came out and wanted to locate the summer range of the caribou that wintered at Poboktan cabin and on the flats at Beauty Creek and the Sunwapta River. We rode the high country from Poboktan Pass to Maligne Pass and into the pass that crosses over to the head of Brazeau Lake. In three days we counted 16 caribou and one grizzly.

In October, another rock school was held in Banff. A trend was developing that influenced the eventual development of the mountain search and rescue unit for each Park. More European mountain specialists were employed by the Park Service and they became the nucleus of each park's search and rescue team. Wardens who had the aptitude for this line of work were given further training and became specialists working with the European climbers. Wardens who failed to meet all expectations and qualifications of this very demanding work were relegated to support services required during a search and rescue.

The rock schools and ski-mountaineering schools continued to provide training for all wardens so they would have a better appreciation of a search and rescue operation. Slowly the division between the advanced climbers and novices widened and everyone knew their role. In this school of 1956 we went from the rock work on Flints Peak to glacier work on Mt. Victoria above Lake Louise to further broaden our experience.

After Christmas we were back in Banff again on a ski-mountaineering school also held at Cuthead College. The emphasis was on avalanche control and search and rescue in the more developed ski areas. We practised bringing an injured patient off a mountain in a sled-type rescue basket while skiing. Runaways were not uncommon during the training period that were extremely dangerous for skier and victim alike but as an observer sometimes hilarious to watch. Skiing had a far greater appeal to most wardens than mountain climbing. As the training continued some very capable and qualified wardens developed into expert skiers.

We missed having a baby in 1956 but not by much. John was born in December, 1955 and Edie was expecting again sometime in February, 1957. I hesitated to take time off and not attend the ski-mountaineering school so we worked out a plan for my absence. Warden Schintz's wife, Glennys and Warden Larry Tremblay's wife Lois, would be staying in Jasper in a vacant government house during the time of the school so Edie made arrangements to move in with them and the children. If the baby came while I was away, there would be someone to take care of the kids and see that Edie made it to the hospital in time.

Baby Thomas Henry Joseph arrived on February 26th while I was somewhere on a mountain miles away. When the school was over I returned to Jasper while Edie was still in the hospital.

In the spring of 1957 there were a number of Chief Warden and Assistant Chief Warden positions coming vacant and would be posted for competition. As a preliminary to filling these positions, a Park Warden Administration Course was held at the Administration Office in Banff. The course content was designed to introduce selected Park Wardens to become familiar with the functions of personnel, finance, adminstration and planning that all were an integral part of the total Park operation. Tom Ross, Murray Dawson and I were sent from Jasper to participate and at the completion of the course, we had to write an exam.

The course lasted two weeks and one day while we were in class, a call came that we had to report to the Temple Ski Lodge as there had been an avalanche on Mt. Richardson. A skier was reported missing. We were fortunate to have all our ski equipment with us in Banff as we intended to spend the weekend skiing.

We met at the ski lodge and continued on to the east slope of Mt. Richardson. Long before we got to the site we could see the slide path. It was a heavy wet spring snow slide that packs solid when it stops sliding. The only clue to where to start looking was a set of ski tracks coming on an angle from the north and heading directly across the slide path. We started a systematic probing line and soon something was detected that felt like a body. On the end of a rescue probe are small barbs and when a searcher detects an object, a twist of the probe will allow the barbs to catch on to any object and bring up a sample.

In this instance it was a few pieces of thread. Digging down we soon found the body packed in solidly. Death was almost surely instant, and the memory I have of that moment was, as I helped lift the body by pulling on the victim's arm was that his watch was still running. Was it a Timex? I don't remember.

The lesson learned which is so often repeated—never ski alone in avalanche country; if you must cross an avalanche slope, cross it high up, take your ski-pole straps off your wrists, put your parka on and do it up, and before you start across, stop and look up and plan an escape route if a slide starts. From what could be seen, this young man had violated every one of these rules.

No sooner had we returned from Banff, March 25, 1957 when we were called out on another search and rescue. The location was east of Jasper and the west side of Brule Lake. Two new Canadians working for the C.N.R. at Brule had a day off and decided to go mountain climbing. They started up a ridge that runs off the south east shoulder of Black Cat Mountain and climbed until they reached a snow-covered bowl. Instead of continuing on up the ridge they decided to traverse the bowl to the other side of the snowfield.

It was still an early spring morning and the sun had not reached the snowfield so the snow was hard-packed and frozen. They had no climbing gear and their footwear consisted of soft-soled shoepack winter boots.

Part way across the frozen basin the slope became steeper and they lost their footing and started sliding down to the edge of an 800 foot cliff. Their momentum carried one man over the cliff and off into space but the other man arrested his fall on a narrow band of exposed rock at the very edge of the cliff where the melting snow had receded. Composing himself, he started to climb up the slope and had almost reached safety when once again he lost his footing and slid back down to the edge of the cliff. Trying once again he slowly and carefully climbed the slope until he reached the safety of the ridge and descended to the station house where he reported the fate of his partner. A request for help came to the Chief Warden in Jasper and he organized the search party.

When we arrived at the station house we were met by the survivor. He accompanied us to the foot of the cliff where the accident took place. It was difficult to fully comprehend what he had to tell us because of his limited ability to speak English. The emotional distress of explaining how he saw his climbing companion go over the cliff and how he also nearly went over himself made it difficult for him to be composed and give us any details.

Searching back and forth across the foot of the cliff we could not locate any trace of the fallen climber and began to doubt the survivor's story. Stopping for tea we gathered together to decide what to do. About this time the sun had cleared the top of the cliff and reached where we were resting. A ray of sun struck a small patch in the snow that caught Warden Larry McGuire's attention a short distance from where we were and he investigated. It was a patch of blood beside a hole in the snow about two feet across but no sign of a body.

Following up on this clue we found further signs that lead us to believe the victim had landed feet first, bounced and continued sliding down a narrow slide path for about 500 feet where we found the remains.

At the annual warden's spring school a competition was posted for a position of Chief Park Warden at Waterton Lake National Park. To win this competition would be a highlight in my career as a Park Warden, especially when it was known how many other of my colleagues were also applying for the same position. After completing a carefully worded application and submitting it to the warden's office, I waited.

When Edie and I were first married and I wanted to return to the Warden Service we made an agreement. If within a period of every five years we considered ourselves locked into a career situation where we were going nowhere it would be time to look for something else. Up until now with the moves we had made we considered it progress. Debbie would be of school age in the fall and we had to resolve how our children were to be educated.

CHAPTER
18
A FISHING TRIP THAT NEARLY ENDED IN DISASTER BUT GOOD NEWS OF A PROMOTION AND NEW COUNTRY TO EXPLORE

WITH the ice leaving the lakes and trout fishing to open soon my fishing partner, Art Day, and I were making plans to check out the hot spots before the tourist season started. Art had been a member of the R.C.M.P. and was replacing Pete Withers at the south gate as the gate attendant for the summer. Pete, when he retired, had given me his fold-boat which was a collapsible kayak before he moved to Little Fort, B.C.

Years before, Pete had been a senior naval officer with the British Navy. Somehow he had invested all his savings in stocks and bonds that were worthless after the great financial collapse of 1929. He came to Jasper and was hired as the district warden for Maligne Lake which was totally out of character for a man of his experience.

The district cabin was located at Maligne Canyon on the hillside across the bridge from where there is now a gift shop. From there, according to Pete, he had to pack all his equipment and supplies to Maligne Lake by horse. By his own admission he knew absolutely nothing about horses and would prefer to walk.

On one occasion he needed to pack a four gallon can of white gas to Maligne Lake for the fire pump. Gas was supplied in square cans with a small handle on top. Pete solved the problem by tying the handle of the can to the front cinch and the horse willingly went to Maligne with the gas suspended between his front legs.

The kayak was to be our way of crossing the Sunwapta River so Art and I could hike into a small lake across the valley from Poboktan cabin. Frank Wells had stocked the Sunwapta River and accordingly fish should have been able to reach the lake where we expected great fishing.

Very early one morning we carried the kayak to the river and on the way I asked Art if he had experienced white water kayaking. "Oh, yes, I did a lot of water travel with the mounties in the north," he replied. We put the kayak in the river with the bow upstream and Art got in the front. I jumped in and immediately Art, with a mighty push, swung the bow out and we were caught broadsides with the rapids rolling us over and over. We both made it to shore and Art thinking it was funny started laughing while I was on my hands and knees trying to catch my breath.

By now the kayak was out of sight down the river with my new rod and reel. We started back for the cabin and by the time we reached there, our outer clothing had frozen. Standing in the kitchen trying to undress and laughing at our misfortune, we woke Edie up. When she looked at us, she couldn't imagine what was so funny as she tried to unfasten frozen buttonholes and peel off frozen clothes.

The kayak hung up on a log jamb and we were able to recover the boat but all the contents were lost. We carried the kayak upstream until we found calmer water and made a successful crossing. With some spare fishing equipment we made the climb up to the lake. The last thing to go wrong, the lake was still frozen over, so we came back home empty-handed.

Towards the end of May a reply came informing me my application was accepted. I went to town for an interview and by the first of June, was offered the position of Chief Warden of Waterton Lakes. Arrangements had to be made to move and by June 18th we were on our way.

Before we left we had to arrange for a new home for the children's pet, Bambi. In the spring of 1956 a tourist had picked up a new-born mule deer fawn on the railroad tracks in Jasper and left it with the Warden Service. A phone call from the warden's office inquired if we would try to raise the fawn at Poboktan. I agreed on the condition that the Park Service would provide milk.

We brought it home and for the first few days it was more demanding than our young son but eventually the three girls took the responsibility of feeding. It had a voracious appetite for milk and the girls scheduled his feeding to when the tour busses from Jasper Park Lodge passed the cabin enroute to the Icefields. As the busses approached, the girls would stand by the roadside and start giving the fawn a bottle. This attracted the tourists and the driver would stop to let them take pictures. Often the girls were rewarded with candy or fruit. One time their picture appeared in the Saturday Evening Post and also featured on the television show, Captain Kangaroo.

For the first few months the deer was easy to handle. As he

(Left) Debbie feeding Bambi.
(Right) Debbie, Suzie and Diane with their cousin Michelle and Auntie Maryanne.

grew older he became very demanding to be fed and would often strike with his front feet. Eventually we quit feeding him and he fended for himself. With the news of our transfer I made arrangements to have him transferred to a game farm.

We stayed at a Bungalow camp the night before we left and had a small gathering of friends for a going-away party. By morning some of the family started to feel ill but we decided to leave anyway. Soon everyone but Diane and I had become terribly sick. It was a constant—"I'm going to throw up!" or "I have to go potty!" Edie would to try and clean up as best she could, using the stack of clean white diapers she had in the car for baby Tom.

We stopped at Waterfowl Lake where it was sunny and a stiff breeze blowing. We spent a couple of hours washing the diapers in the creek and draping them over the willow brush to dry. With a change of clothing, everyone was clean again and feeling somewhat better, we continued on to Banff. After checking in at the Pinewood Bungalows for the night we thought it best to call a doctor especially for Suzanne who still appeared very sick. In the doctor's opinion she should feel better by morning.

The next day we loaded up and were on our way without breakfast. At Calgary there was some interest in eating so we stopped at the Crossroads Cafe, which was an appropriate name for us as we felt we were at the crossroads of a new experience in our lives. We never failed to remember our ordeal of moving to Waterton every time we drove past the distinctive globe at the top of this hotel.

At Fort McLeod we turned west following the Old Man River and from the view we had of the valley in full bloom and the mountains in the distance we knew we would love our new home. The first surprise when we reached Waterton was a fully modern house to live in located directly across the road from a school house.

Within hours of starting my new job a lightning strike started a forest fire at timberline on Vimy Mountain giving me my first supervisory experience as a Chief Park Warden. It was like "being a new kid on the block," and you were being tested by staff.

Coming up from the ranks to a position of authority above men who were your comrades a few weeks before can be difficult. One resident warden was disappointed he had not been selected for the position; another had been reclassified from the position of a Chief Warden from another Park; still another had been a Chief Warden in the north and had taken a demotion to come south. The fourth was a career warden who had spent all of 30 years in Waterton, and the youngest was a feisty newcomer to the service who contested nearly everything that was suggested to him to do.

Eventually we all worked out our problems and developed a good working relationship. I was fortunate to have as the office warden a man who had been a district warden before a serious car accident left him a paraplegic and confined to a wheel chair. Leonard Gladstone, a descendant of the distinguished Senator Gladstone, and a native of the Waterton area was a wealth of information on all features of the Park.

The traditional First of July parade in Waterton was well organized, colourful and impressive with Red Coated Mounties and Indians in full dress riding in the lead. The event attracted many Albertans and Americans from the Glacier National Park area. Planning to go to the parade Edie stopped unpacking, and realizing the stroller was broken, was thinking she'd have to carry the baby in her arms. Then she remembered the mossbag which she had unpacked already and strapped little four-month old Tom into it and off the six of them went to see the parade on the main street. The wardens and I were also riding horses in the parade and I saw her taking pictures of this exciting event.

As she walked along beside the parade she noticed a following of camera buffs close behind. They were snapping pictures of her, with her little brood of young children and Tom, with his mop of straight black hair and black shining eyes, smiling at everyone pointing at him. When the reporter from the Hungry Horse News in Columbia Falls, Montana wrote up the illustrated story of the parade, Edie and Tom were featured on the front page.

Although the park is small by comparison to many other

national parks, its location is one of the most picturesque settings in the Rockies. The Indians referred to the area as Okok-si-kimi meaning beautiful waters, or the land of shining mountains. The mountains rise abruptly from the prairie grasslands. A network of trails lead to numerous alpine lakes and over high mountain passes. Glacier National Park, Montana adjoins Waterton to the south and the British Columbia border to the west giving the park unique features of a transition zone for flora and fauna not found anywhere else along the eastern slope of the Rockies.

Acquainting myself with the Park was part of my job and my curiosity to explore new country led me to the Kintla Lakes in Glacier National Park. Ray Woodward was a seasonal warden and agreed to go with me on a pack-trip to the Kintla, Kishinena and Akamina watersheds. Leaving Cameron Lake we crossed Akamina Pass and climbed to Wall Lake. Above Wall Lake a high pass crosses a summit to the headwaters of the north Kintla River where we expected to find a trail near a nunnatuk, (nunatak, in some dictionaries), that stands in the centre of a high alpine basin.

Unable to pick up any sign of a trail, we continued downstream following the water course. Soon we were in fallen timber and the horses were having a terrible time. The three pack horses were constantly getting hung up trying to jump over windfallen trees and often had to be rescued by chopping a log to free them. By evening we were still travelling in an easterly direction which indicated to us we had yet to cross the International border.

Finding a small sandbar on the creek where we had room to camp, we unpacked the horses and tied them up for the night knowing there wasn't any place for them to graze. Before going to sleep we agreed we were not making any progress and in the morning would proceed on foot to try and find a trail. We hung up all our gear and saddlery in a cache and turned the horses loose to fend for themselves. With a small survival pack we left looking for a way out of this entanglement. Within a half hour we were out on a newly cleared trail on the boundary.

We chopped our way back to the campsite. Fortunately the horses hadn't pulled out so we packed up and rode to the lower end of Kintla Lakes. The next day we went north-west to the Ranger's cabin on Starvation Creek and continued up the Kishinena Creek to the International Boundary where we camped. A day's ride from there following the Kishinena and Akamina Creeks to Akamina Pass brought us home.

WATERTON LAKES NATIONAL PARK WILDLIFE MANAGEMENT PROGRAMS AND PROBLEMS, AND ANDY RUSSELL'S SCEPTICISM ON SOME OF MY PROJECTS

THE annual migration of elk was usually regulated by weather conditions. The summer range for one large herd was at the headwaters of the Belly River in Glacier National Park. The winter range was in Waterton Lakes along the east slope of the mountains. In severe winter weather, the herd moved on to the ranch lands east of Waterton and wreaked havoc with the rancher's hay stacks and pastures. With three options the elk were at liberty to take, it provided the American, Canadian and Alberta provincial governments an opportunity to disclaim any responsibility for the problems created by the elk.

When the elk moved out to the ranchlands and started feeding on haystacks, the elk hunters would appear overjoyed at the chance to shoot the elk. The rancher considered the elk hunter as great a menace as the elk, leaving gates open, random shooting and violating "no trespassing and no hunting signs." Provincial authorities passed these complaints on to the National Parks stating that the Parks harboured and protected the elk except during severe winter months.

Waterton National Park built elk traps baited with hay and when conditions permitted trapped and shot hundreds of elk. The disposal of the meat and hides was the same as in other Parks. The Indians in Southern Alberta were the recipients but considered it their aboriginal right to hunt the elk themselves in the Park. Fish and Game associations wanted the Park to have a lottery and allow resident Albertans to hunt in the Park. In turn the Park authorities hoped for an early spring when the elk returned to their summer range in Glacier National Park where they gave birth to the next generation.

In the fall the cycle would start all over again with never a satisfactory resolution that would be a compromise for all concerned. Some cattlemen took the position that if Park elk could forage on rangeland, what was wrong with cattle grazing in the Park? When the wardens rounded up the cattle and impounded them until the impounding fee was paid, it was like waving a red flag in front of a bull.

Another year and we expected another baby in the spring. This pregnancy was creating many complications and often required a fast trip to the doctor or hospital in Pincher Creek, 35 miles away. As long as the road was good it didn't take long to make the trip but with snow and strong winds the road could close within the hour. To help prevent a miscarriage the doctor administered a new drug called stilbesterol that probably saved the baby. Stilbesterol later proved to be a mixed blessing as at the age of puberty, girls sometimes developed cancer of the reproductive organs. A healthy baby boy, Ross Joseph was born April 14, 1958. We're thankful to family and friends who looked after some of the other children during this trying time.

A plan by the Canadian Wildlife Service was proposed to try and collect accurate information on the Bighorn sheep population in the Park. A trap was built on the lower slopes of Avion Ridge above the road to Red Rock Canyon and baited with salt. In the spring before the sheep moved to higher ground they frequented the salt lick. When a number of sheep were in the trap, a warden posted as lookout would spring the gate enclosing the sheep. A crew of usually five wardens would approach the trapped sheep and herd them into a small holding pen. The pen was a darkened shed which had a settling effect on the sheep. A trap door from the pen opened into a chute and when a sheep came through the trap door the chute would be compressed to steady the animal. A blindfold pulled over the sheep's head to cover the eyes would immediately subdue the sheep and the necessary information would be recorded. Age, weight, sex, girth, and length of horn and leg measurements completed the exam. A numbered tag secured to an ear identified each animal and could be read from a distance with binoculars for later observations. The horns were given a coat of bright red paint to further distinguish the marked sheep from the unmarked sheep when they dispersed into different bands on the summer range.

As the program was repeated each year more accurate information was recorded. Yearlings trapped in the first one or two years and later caught again would give detailed actual growth for that period. With older animals there was a possibility of error in determining age. Reported sightings by the wardens from various locations gave an indication of the sheep migration during the summer.

The credibility of one statistic to determine population in the relationship of marked sheep counted in a band of unmarked sheep was questionable. Nearly all reports stated that for every marked sheep at least four unmarked sheep were counted. By now we had marked over 150 individual sheep which according to the reports represented one in five, or twenty percent of the total population or at least 750 sheep in the Park. No one agreed with this extrapolation because at no time had the wardens been able to observe in total that many sheep. There must be many reasons for this discrepancy that have not been studied and analyzed. The initial purposes of the project was never fully attained.

One day Diane asked me for help on a school project that required data collecting and using graphs to demonstrate trends. I gave her the basic information on the sheep we had surveyed in relation to sex, age and size of horn. This I thought would be enough to record variables. When she was finished I reviewed what she had done and was surprised to note a statistic I hadn't expected.

Female sheep showed a progressive growth in horn length and a circumference until prime at ages seven and eight and then a decline in measurements as they got older. At the same time male sheep continued to increase their horn size as they matured. I showed this information to a biologist who gave it a cursory review and passed it over as inconclusive.

An incident that nearly ended my career happened when we were trying to chase some old mature rams into the holding pen by running behind and crowding them at the pen entrance. They decided they weren't going to be penned and turned around to run by us. For some reason I thought I could bulldog one as he went by. At the same time another ram butted me from behind.

The impact sent me into the air and I was carried along for about forty feet before landing on the ground unconscious. When I came to, four wardens were standing by looking concerned but when I moved and showed signs of life they broke out in gales of laughter. I guess the image I displayed could have had serious consequences but was also very funny. The pattern of my underwear was imprinted on my rear in the form of a colourful bruise for days later.

All these questionable game management projects came under the scrutiny and watchful eye of Andy Russell, who lived just outside the Park on a picturesque hill called the Hawks Nest. Andy was becoming a self-professed naturalist conservationist and was writing a book titled "Grizzly Country." He spent many hours in and around Waterton Lakes National Park photographing wildlife and recording his observations.

Another book he was preparing to write was "Horns In The High Country," that presented a "many-sided view of wild sheep and the natural world in which they live." There wasn't much "wildness" in sheep that had been trapped, ear-tagged and horns painted red and Andy let us know in no uncertain words what he thought about it all. In retrospect he was probably right for when all this information was correlated the natural behaviour of sheep remained unchanged.

Edie and I had ridden over Carthew Summit from the Cameron Lake side and just beside the Carthew Lakes we saw Andy and his sons glassing the mountains. They had a movie camera set up to record a colony of pikas. As we spoke Andy commented on the difficulty of ever photographing a wolverine feeding on a sheep.

We continued on towards Alderson Lake when I saw a wolverine feeding on a carcass at the foot of an old avalanche. I rode back and alerted Andy and continued on home. Andy checked the site and the wolverine was still feeding on what was a mule deer carcass. The next time we met, Andy related the whole story to me.

Early next morning there was evidence of a grizzly having fed on the carcass overnight but as the movie camera crew watched, the wolverine returned. An unusual observation was made. The wolverine would take a piece of meat, carry it to a small stream and wash it before eating and then repeat the same routine.

The bears of Waterton were no different than the bears of Jasper—they loved their garbage. Residents and visitors alike paid little attention to the bears unless for some reason they were affected personally. Soon after I arrived in Waterton I received a phone call from a summer resident living on the "back" street who told me to get up to her place and do something about a mother and three cubs that were taking over her back yard. I was also told if nothing was done "now," she would get her husband, a lawyer to sue the Park Service. I talked to one of the wardens who was familiar with the problems summer residents felt the Park staff failed to resolve, but were seldom prepared to make any changes themselves to help.

I went up to the house and the bears were still tearing the place apart scavenging for garbage. I shot the mother and the three cubs. The repercussions that bounced from that incident had lasting effects. The woman who wanted action "now" complained I shouldn't have killed the bears, just chase them away. My defence was, cleanup the garbage or put up with bears, you can't have it both ways. The Lethbridge newspaper made an issue of the incident, which brought on more controversy. Eventually the Park Service built an incinerator to burn the garbage and the residents co-operated in keeping their garbage out of reach of bears.

Bears had a good selection of places to hibernate in the town for the winter. Many of the seasonal cottages were poorly constructed and some crawl spaces were left open. This provided a dry comfortable place to curl up for the winter and in the spring it wasn't too difficult to find an easy handout.

The owner of the local dance hall asked me to remove a bear from beneath the dance hall because the bear was building his winter bed out of the insulation around the pipes and the pipes would freeze. I set the bear trap and before the bear hibernated, took the bait and was caught.

When I went to move the bear trap the owner asked if he could come with me to dispose of the bear. The method of disposal was primitive, you opened the trap door at a selected site, and when the bear jumped out, he was shot. On the way out the question was asked, "What if this bear showed up without his hide?" There would be hell to pay, I replied. We disposed of the bear and returned to town. I asked the duty warden that evening to check the bear. As I half-expected the bear had been skinned. Back to the dance hall, I proceeded to search and found a fresh black bear pelt. I charged the dance hall owner with the illegal possession of the hide.

On the day of the trial, the son of the accused who was a lawyer in Lethbridge represented his father. In a most abusive and flourishing grandstand display of small town courtroom drama, the lawyer did everything to intimidate and embarrass me. Judge McLeod was presiding, and with forty years of experience on the bench, was not convinced of the accused's innocence and found him guilty.

Following the trial, there was a social gathering before the lawyer left for Lethbridge. When leaving town he ran off the road and couldn't be located until the next day. In the car was an unsealed firearm that was seized and charges were laid against the lawyer for illegal possession of an unsealed firearm. Back in court again the lawyer was found guilty, fined and his firearm held for six months.

In the winter of 1958 the wardens were introduced to a new mechanical device called an autotoboggan, the forerunner to the modern ski-doo. I had seen a demonstration in Riding Mountain National Park earlier that winter on a frozen lake and it was very impressive.

In the mountains it was impossible to operate. With the length over eleven feet it required a wide circle to change direction. The track was pivoted on the front driving axle and in loose snow the back of the track dropped to about a 30 degree angle. Unless conditions were ideal, most of the day was spent pushing or pulling the machine out of the snow. The idea that this would be a labour-saving device was soon abandoned.

Corp. Ralph Thompson and myself introducing the new system of a self sealing gun station to a visitor, Waterton, 1964.

Al Oeming from the Alberta Game Farm showed up one day with a permit to trap four mule deer does and take them to his Game Farm. I had been following Al's career for years after the war and was never surprised what enterprise he was working on next. Al and a friend of his, Stu Hart from Calgary, had enlisted in the navy the same day as I had in Edmonton in February 1944. We took basic training at the same time and were together in Cornwallis for advanced training. From there we parted company until after the war.

Al and Stu were body building enthusiasts and were continually training for the day they could enter the wrestling ring as a tag team. They got their chance in the States after the war but their career ended abruptly when Al had his leg broken during a match. Al decided to be a wrestling promoter and his first promoted fight in Edmonton was poorly attended. The referee's decision was biased and a fight broke out in the small crowd. It turned into a riot with coke bottles busted on heads and the next morning made headlines. For the next match the crowd was bigger hoping for another riot but they were satisfied with the match and Al's career was away.

With the proceeds he went to university, drove a Cadillac and got a degree in zoology. Next came the Alberta Game Farm and with many negotiations around the world obtained an outstanding variety of first class specimens for his farm.

His reason for being in Waterton was to capture four does that hopefully were pregnant. We asked for assistance from Dave Simpson who was handy with a lasso. Quietly selecting the deer we wanted and walking up close enough for Dave to throw his lasso, the deer were captured. The following spring Al phoned to tell me the four does had been pregnant and two gave birth to twin fawns and two one fawn each.

20

A HUNTING TRIP TO THE BRAZEAU AND BACK TO WATERTON LAKES AND MORE ADVENTURES

D AVE Simpson bought out Andy Russell's guiding and out-fitting business in Waterton and became successful in the Horses For Hire enterprise. His outgoing personality and venturesome outlook on new challenges made him an interesting person. After telling him of the hunting opportunities in the Brazeau River area, we decided to go and have a look. By limiting our supplies and equipment we managed to pack everything on one horse.

We left Waterton with an old horse trailer loaded with two horses and another horse in the truck. Our destination was Camp Parker on the Banff-Jasper Highway. Leaving the truck and trailer we packed up and followed the trail over Nigel Pass. Over the Pass we turned up Cataract Creek and soon I was in unfamiliar country. My plan was to cross Cataract Pass, go down the Cline River to MacDonald Creek, up MacDonald Creek and over an unnamed summit to the headwaters of Job Creek where I expect-ed we would find goat and caribou.

Without too much concern about where we would camp, we reached MacDonald Creek and started climbing into the high country. Somehow we took the wrong fork in the creek and ended up on top of a mountain called Afternoon Peak looking down on to the south fork of the Brazeau. I was completely dis-oriented until I picked up some familiar landmarks around the Brazeau Headquarters cabin.

Time was spent glassing over the country as we had crossed caribou tracks before reaching the summit. Afternoon Peak was certainly an appropriate name at the moment for us. It was late afternoon and it had been a long day since we left Camp Parker.

We gave up the idea of trying to find Job Creek so headed

down the mountain side towards the Brazeau River. The going was steep and part way down the pack horse lost his footing.

After turning a cartwheel he came to rest near some small trees unhurt but the pack had rolled and had to be repacked. For some reason we found this whole absurdity hilarious and could hardly pack the poor horse between our fits of laughter. What triggered this moment of hilarity was a box of Kellogg's Corn Flakes that had fallen out of the packbox. The packhorse had rolled over the box flattening it to a pancake thickness. When Dave picked it up to repack it, the appearance of the box summarized our predicament and released our pent-up frustrations. We made it to the valley bottom and camped.

The next day we stayed on the Park trail to the mouth of Job Creek, crossed the river and camped. For the next few days we hunted up Job Creek and I was lucky enough to shoot a goat. When we left for home we decided to take the scenic route over Poboktan Pass and out to the highway by Poboktan cabin.

At home in Waterton the family was enjoying the amenities of living in a small community. The multigrade school house was exactly what we *A nostalgic return to the Brazeau cabin.* needed for all our children to obtain their primary education. Located directly across the road from our house, it was convenient for the kids to come and go with their friends. In one baking session Edie would make twelve dozen Spudnuts or twelve dozen cookies hoping they'd last a week but sometimes by suppertime they'd have nearly all disappeared.

With the problems Edie had in carrying Ross to term we were concerned about having more children but after a year's rest we were expecting our seventh child. There were a few panic trips to the doctor and hospital but on June 17, 1960 a healthy baby boy joined our family. We named him David Joseph for David Simpson.

With seven children in eight years and two miscarriages in between it was time to consider our future. The work already would add up to ten consecutive years of daily diaper washing and our budget was at a point of deficit financing.

A new olympic-size swimming pool had been built in the middle of the village and provided an opportunity for the kids to spend time and learn how to swim. Bernice Coward was the lifeguard and lived with us during the summers. As an olympic competitor in gymnastics and swimming instructor, her association with us in a family setting provided an excellent role model for the kids.

The church also provided a centre for family activity. The parish priest, Father Paul Grueter, had an outgoing personality that was always appealing and combined with his sincerity, had us all involved in church activities. Next door to the Catholic church was the Lion Community hall, a focal point of many community functions. Dances, parties, Christmas concerts, Guides and Brownies, Scouts and Cubs, weddings, funerals and any other reason for a group to gather used the Lions Hall.

Hiking and camping as a family was always a way to spend a holiday that was both exciting and inexpensive. My sister Maryanne, her husband, Frank, and their four children would visit and we would take off on some great adventure. One summer with two packhorses loaded with supplies, we left the Snowshoe cabin near the Castle River Divide and headed for Lone Lake. Camping at the lake everyone did their own thing. Fishing, hiking, reading or looking after the campfire were all part of the experience. One of the greatest thrills was glissading down snowfields in the bright warm sunshine. A comparable thrill today would probably be watersliding.

With any group of young children, eating outdoors is also a high priority activity and soon we were running out of food and with one of the boys developing a severe allergy from the horses we started home. The dilemma was to get him home riding a horse or hike in his weakened condition. The solution was to divide his time between walking and riding. With eleven kids ages eleven and under we always anticipated some crisis on our hiking or camping trips.

I thought of another young boy on a hike up Vimy mountain when we first arrived in Waterton who wasn't so lucky. The group had been staying at one of the youth camps in the Park and had gone on an overnight hike on the east slope of Vimy Mountain. During the night the young boy got sick and part way down the next morning was too ill to continue. His comrades bedded him under a windfallen tree and told him they were going for help. Instead of leaving someone with the sick boy they all came back to the camp to report the boy's sickness to the camp supervisor. The wardens were called to help in the rescue and went back up the mountain with some of the group. When they reached the approximate site, no one could recall the exact place they had left their companion. The first day's searching failed to find the boy and it wasn't until later the next day that his body was found. A lesson learned the hard way. If someone had stayed with him he would have been found sooner and may have survived.

In the late 1800's along the banks of Cameron Creek, four and one half miles above Cameron Falls, oil seeped to the surface and was collected by early settlers to lubricate wagons. Then in 1901 two local promoters sold shares and formed a company. They drilled at the same location and called the site Oil City. They struck oil at about 1000 feet and over a period of five years had only produced about 750 gallons. The company dissolved but other promoters went over Akamina Pass and continued their search for more oil. Another well was sunk on Sage Creek and out of curiosity I decided to take a trip from Waterton to have a look.

Ray Woodward agreed to make the trip with me and this time Edie accompanied us. With three packhorses and our saddle horses we went from Red Rock Canyon over the South Kootenay Pass and tried to follow the old original Indian trail down Sage Creek. The trail had grown in and was hard to find. What was a virgin and pristine timbered valley has today been completely destroyed by timber harvesting.

At one point Edie's horse fell over backwards and Edie landed on her back, luckily on a rotten log. The log broke her fall and not her back, thank God.

We camped in a meadow about ten miles below the pass and the next day reached the well site. The old wooden derrick was still standing and in a shack nearby lived an old couple, Joe and Mrs. MacDonald. We stopped for tea and picked up some of the local history.

Charlie Wise had been a trapper in the area for many years and still lived in a shack at the U.S. boundary crossing on the Flathead River. Charlie had built a cabin out of some large logs along the Kishinena River and in the early days lived there with his wife and young daughter. One winter his daughter swallowed a button that lodged in her throat and was having difficulty breathing. Charlie snowshoed out to Columbia Falls over 50 miles away, carrying her on his back. His daughter died and in a few days Charlie went back to his cabin. When he arrived home he found his wife dead in bed. She had apparently died from the flu.

On our return trip home we stopped at the cabin site and took pictures. We found the trail Ray and I had travelled on our return trip from Kintla Lakes and followed it to Akamina Pass and home.

The next year, Frank and Lenore Goble took Edie and me on a Jeep trip through the Crowsnest Pass to Corbin, then south along the Flathead River to Columbia Falls, Montana. At the International boundary we stopped and met Charlie Wise who was a friend of Frank's and Lenore's. Charlie was a very gracious host and over a cup of coffee recalled his early days as a trapper. From Columbia Falls we returned over the Going To The Sun Highway and through the Chief Mountain customs port of entry to Waterton.

The "Bear's Hump," the cliff overlooking the village is a one mile hike rising 800 feet giving a commanding view of the lakes and prairie for miles around. It was always a favourite place to take our youngsters and visitors to show off our beautiful scenery. When the west wind was blowing, the kids sat with their feet anchored in a crevice to keep them from going over the cliff. Warden Jack Christiansen grew up in Waterton and often talked about how when he was young with his friends would spend days packing old tires to the top of the Bear's Hump. Then one by one they would start the tires rolling over the cliff in the direction of the village. Tires falling from that height and then bouncing near the base of the cliff would sometimes clear the main road and land in the lake. He didn't say if any tires hit one of the homes. If they had, it wasn't because of concern when they pushed them over the side.

Dave Simpson and I were discussing the probability of riding a horse to the top of the Bear's Hump. Dave was interested in the feasibility of pony traffic to the summit. We saddled up two good horses and started the climb. The lower part of the trail was easy but near the summit, it was a scramble to jump up some of the rock ledges. Once on top we took pictures to record the climb. Whether we were the first to ride horses to the top we never knew but concluded it wasn't a very necessary exercise to repeat.

Lineham Lakes, named after one of the oil promoters at Oil City, were located in a high mountain valley inaccessible to most people visiting the Park. The trail up Lineham Creek ended abruptly at the foot of a cliff below the lakes. To get over the cliff a rock climb up the left side was necessary. Up the right side, one had to climb a talus slope and traverse along a narrow ledge which had an inclining slope to the outer edge. Neither approach was suitable for the faint of heart. It was a credit to the early day wardens who back-packed live fish over this cliff in containers with water to initially stock the lakes.

An alternate route was passed Rowe Lakes and over a mountain summit separating the Rowe Lakes from the Lineham Lakes and descending into the Lineham basin. Andy Russell pioneered this route and Dave Simpson occasionally had fishing parties who reached the lakes this way. On one of Dave's trips I accompanied his party and was impressed with the degree of effort some fishermen go to when they are looking for a good place to fish. It's a tough place to get in and out of but the fishing was excellent.

21

WATERTON, 1964
WIND, RAIN AND FLOODS
BANFF PROMOTION

IN the winter of 1963-64 heavy snow fell in the mountains and spring was late in arriving. On June 7, 1964 a heavy warm rain began to fall melting the snow in the high country. The snowmelt and rain combined produced flooding conditions on Cameron Creek. The next morning the creek overflowed its banks and soon many homes and cottages were being flooded. Our home was in the mainstream of the flood and it was necessary to evacuate. The manager of the Prince of Wales opened the doors of the hotel to people in the community needing sleeping accommodation and meals. Within 36 hours the level of the lake had risen nine and one half feet. The buildings along the lakeshore had water up to the eaves. The main street was under water and all businesses had to be closed.

The wardens were kept busy ensuring the safety of everyone, especially those who tried to return to their homes before the flood subsided. In some instances older residents elected to stay with their possessions. The park entrance road at the Park gate was also under water and persons wishing to leave the Park were escorted through the flooded road.

Our own home flooded with water flowing by at the level of the windowboxes. The doors had sealed as they absorbed the water and the main floor received only minor water damage. We had moved most of our possessions out of the basement so suffered little damage as the water poured in through the basement windows rising to the ceiling. The current of water flowing around the basement footing dug a deep hole on the downstream side of the house and when the flood subsided we found a dead moose. Where once our garden and lawn had been was now a dry gravel stream bed.

Some homes were moved from their foundations by the force of the flood waters. Many propane storage tanks were torn from their bases and could be seen floating out in the lake. The sewage pumping stations went underwater and failed. It was nearly ten days before the community started to recover and during this time all the children who were billeted at the Prince of Wales were having a great time. School was closed and the hotel provided a holiday atmosphere. A great deal of credit was given to the management and staff of the hotel to put up with this inconvenience especially when they were preparing for a busy summer tourist season.

This natural disaster was followed by another natural disaster in the fall. A violent wind storm approached from the northwest and in a sudden lull, the trees whipped back and were blown over. It was hard to comprehend why most of the trees fell in the direction the wind came from. Trees in a total of 670 acres and five locations were windfallen. A salvage operation recovered some of the timber on the north slope of Blakiston Mountain. A trailer camp was set up and a crew of 75 natives from the Blackfoot Indian Reserves were employed in the operation.

By 1964 we had lived in Waterton for nearly seven years. The older girls would need to be bussed out of the village to Cardston to attend school next year. I was getting restless and much of my work was repetitious. A higher classification for my position was unlikely so I decided to upgrade my qualifications with the expectation for new job opportunities.

A Junior Officer Training Course was offered and I enroled. It was a correspondence course that required a year and a half to complete. Every ten days I submitted a paper on whatever administrative subject the course content covered in that time period. A mentor in Ottawa reviewed the paper, made comments and gave it a graded value. The course placed as great a demand on Edie's time as it did on mine. With her previous business and office training the secretarial requirements were passed on to her. I never did master typing or spelling.

At the completion of the course and with acceptable marks I went to Ottawa to attend a three week course of government administration and orientation of the headquarters operation. To give time to detach myself from the demanding routine of homelife with seven children interrupting any attempt to concentrate, I decided to travel by train from Calgary to Ottawa. This would give me three days of quiet time to read and prepare for the weeks ahead. The plan was sound but it failed. I found the sleeper-car and my assigned berth when a harried mother and three pre-school children entered and sat beside me. Her destination was Ottawa.

The Ottawa exposure and tempo made the adjustment of coming back to work in Waterton unsettling. There was no assurance that all this training would ever be applied in a new job situation. I didn't have long to wait. Just before Christmas, 1965 I was offered a position as a Program Administrator in Banff National Park and accepted.

Winter time in the mountains is not the most ideal season to transfer to a new job. Moving between Christmas and New Year's only compounded the problem except it was a school break and would give the children a few days to adjust to their new home. The moving van driver gave us the impression he disagreed with working during the holidays especially when he got his rig stuck in a snowbank trying to reach the house.

Strong winds blowing off the frozen lake carried snow on to the town-site. The drifts that were created were often as high as the houses which made for great recreation for the kids. It also gave the deer an opportunity to walk to the top of a snowdrift and feed on the tender needles of the conifer trees. In the summertime after the snow had melted, visitors would enquire why the trees had been trimmed to such height and a casual response would be, "Oh, the deer do that." This would be viewed with disbelief until you explained the deer had been feeding from the top of a snowbank.

The one feature of Waterton that we would not miss were the winds. When strong Chinook winds blew from the west the velocity was sometimes recorded in excess of 100 miles an hour. A person's residency in the community was determined by what he did when he lost his hat. If he went chasing after it he was a newcomer. If he stood by and caught the next hat passing him, he was an old-timer.

When we arrived in Banff, we checked in at the Cascade Hotel as our furniture had not arrived. We suspected the driver was making his point about working during the holiday by celebrating New Year's Eve somewhere along the way. Staying in downtown Banff in the busy holiday season and eating in restaurants was fun for the kids but an ordeal for Edie and me.

Each day we went to the vacant house, the old fish hatchery residence, lit a fire in the fireplace and waited. Days later when the van arrived the driver, attempting to back up to unload was once again stuck in a snow bank. With the help of the older kids, we packed our possessions to the house and the heavier items, including a piano, were hauled in on a toboggan.

Soon we were settled and the children enroled in school. I reported for work in the position of Visitor Services Supervisor. I was now part of the Banff National Park executive group. You were expected to report promptly for work each morning in a clean, starched white shirt and tie, a change from a warden's uniform.

The Visitor Services activity included the operation of campgrounds, swimming pools, picnic areas, Park entrance gateways, janitorial services, information centres, food, boat and horse concessions, and the adminstration of contracts with the public sector for some campground operations.

The total number of staff during the peak summer season would be over four hundred supervised by first-line managers who reported to me directly. The diversity of activities, the interaction with park visitors and their problems or concerns made the job interesting. The fact that you could walk out of your office at quitting time and be very seldom interrupted on your own time was a welcome change from the demanding and expected response of a call-out as a warden.

It was the family's good fortune to move to Banff at this point in our lives. School provided so many opportunities for each child to progress with children their own age. Recreational activities were so varied that there was something of interest for everyone. Part-time summer jobs for students helped to finance individual special interests. Edie worked in a post card shop for a season and then as an Expeditor for the Department of Public Works. Her schedule allowed time to be with the children when they were home. It was also a time for her to break away from the demanding life of a mother and homemaker for part of the day and re-enter the world of adults. The Banff School of Fine Arts provided an opportunity to pursue her interest in art sponsored by the Community Art Society.

Most of my time was confined to the office but once I became familiar with my duties, I took the time to travel to some of the outlying areas of the Park. A trip up Healy Creek to Monarch Ridge with the older children gave me a chance to find Bill Peyto's old prospector cabin. Built in about 1916 the cabin was still in good shape and appeared as if no change had taken place since that period of time. Food in old cans was still in the cupboard, detonator caps for blasting were in a small square red tin on the table, clothes hung on pegs on the wall and there was a pile of dry firewood in the anteroom. I wondered why such a historical building was not given some protection.

Warden Andy Anderson was going into the Red Deer Lakes and invited Edie and me to come along. There was still snow on the trail above Temple Lodge but once in the Red Deer River valley it was like summer. We had hoped the fishing would be good but it turned out to be excellent. Andy knew the secret, but first we had to catch the first fish, which landed in at about three pounds. Without explaining himself he cut up the fish into chunks and told us to bait our hooks. Baiting Edie's first, she made a cast and caught a fish. After helping her land a two pounder, I baited her hook, another cast and another fish. We soon had more than enough fish for supper and I hadn't even had a chance to try my luck. Next morning we repeated the previous night's routine and soon had our limit to take back to town.

In Waterton Dave Simpson had given the kids a young colt which was now three years old. I borrowed a truck and went back to Waterton to bring "Thunder" to Banff. We stabled him at the community corrals which was about three miles from our house. The daily demands to care and feed the animal were as great a burden as trying to schedule who would take Thunder for exercise and training.

Moose hunting season opened so I borrowed two horses from Warden "Dixie" Dougan at Healy Creek. With a truck and trailer, I hauled Thunder and the two other horses up the Banff-Jasper highway to the trail head for Sunset Pass. Once over the pass I was out of the Park and camped at Pinto Lake. During the day I'd leave my campsite and go down to the Cline River hoping to find a moose or elk and return to Pinto Lake for the night. I left Thunder tied up in camp one day as he wouldn't follow along unless he was lead. Returning to camp I found the halter still tied to the tree and Thunder missing. For two days I looked for him, gave up and returned to Banff. Ted Stafford, the Park radio technician, had a plane and I told him if he could locate the horse from the air he could have him. After an air search without finding the horse we stopped looking. The next spring Bert Mickle who had the Lake Louise horse concession told me he had seen Thunder at the Ermineskin Indian camp on the Kootenay Plains.

One weekend, using a horse trailer I had built, I drove down the David Thompson highway to the Ermineskin camp. A few Indians were standing by and I explained to them I had come to pick up my horse. I pointed to the black gelding standing in the corral with the other horses. No one disagreed with my choice and I haltered him and loaded him into the trailer. In Banff I saw Ted Stafford and told him he could have the horse. Ted took time to break Thunder to pull a sulky and over the years took prizes in competition.

CHAPTER

22

BANFF – A NEW CAREER
BETWEEN A ROCK AND
A HARD PLACE

CCEPTING the position as Visitor Services Officer in Banff
had the advantage of a reclassification that could lead to
further promotions, but it also required accepting direct
supervision under the Superintendent, Harry Dempster.

Harry Dempster's administrative style was to keep subordi-
nates in total fear, assuming maximum productivity would be
achieved. You spent as much time looking over your shoulder as
planning ahead so you took every opportunity to leave the office
and do something less stressful. In the fall I took my holidays and
went to Jasper to work for Tom McCready as a packer-horse
wrangler on a hunting trip north of the Park. The outfit was at
Tom's base camp at Rock Lake. The first day out we rode up Rock
Creek, through the Park and camped at a site called Mile 58.
From Mile 58 we crossed a high shoulder of a mountain to our
west and on to the south fork of the Sulphur River. A base camp
was set up and for a few days Tom hunted the mountains nearby.
One of the hunters shot a goat and then we moved camp down
the Sulphur to a site just below Little Grave, an Indian burial site.
We stayed at this camp for the rest of the hunt while the two
hunters and guides fly-camped in the different high valleys within a day's travel. The cook and I had time to ride the different
trails and explore the surrounding country.

A sightseeing trip to the summit of Rocky Pass was spoiled
by a large dump of empty red painted gas barrels left by a survey
party that had worked the area with a helicopter. It's unfortunate
this type of pollution could not be controlled. The barrels will be
there for years destroying the aesthetic value of these mountains.

Another trip was down the Sulphur River to Big Grave Flats,
another Indian burial site. We checked at the Forest Ranger sta-

tion but the building looked abandoned. Crossing the river I was looking for a trapper cabin that Louis Joachim told me about years ago that belonged to him. I found it in heavy timber back on a bench away from the river.

After the second hunter had shot a caribou he was satisfied so we packed up and moved out to Rock Lake and Jasper.

I had been away from the ski scene for eight winters but after a few weekends some of my skill returned. Nearly every weekend was spent on the slopes and as we equipped some of the kids with skis they were always anxious to spend their free time skiing.

Wednesday afternoons free ski lessons were given to the women by the ski patrol. Edie rounded up what fit her from the children's equipment and joined other mothers for their afternoon on the slopes. The frustrations of being an infrequent skier with ill-fitting equipment was tempered by an afternoon drink of gluewein.

The Park had started a program of erecting high alpine shelters for public use. Brian Lemke, a park engineer, Bert Darling, the accountant from Yoho, and I planned a spring ski touring trip from Bow Summit to the Kicking Horse River. We left Bow Summit and dropped down to Peyto Lake and went up the Peyto Glacier to an alpine hut I think was called the "David Thompson." The next day we climbed until we could traverse the Bow Glacier and work our way over to Hector Glacier above Hector Lake. By mid-afternoon the weather closed in on us and we travelled on a compass bearing hoping to find the Hector alpine hut. This was all new territory for us and after awhile we began to wonder if we were off our compass bearing and had skied passed the hut. It seemed unlikely so we agreed to continue on our course. Luckily we did because within another half hour we caught a glimpse of a small patch of orange colour. The hut was straight ahead and the orange patch was a section of the dome where the snow had fallen off. At daylight we were on the trail climbing the crest of Hector Glacier and carried on into the watershed of the Yoho valley. Soon the valley narrowed and it was with some hesitation that we continued on for fear of avalanches. Taking every precaution and with only one skier at a time we crossed each potential avalanche slope until we were in better and safer conditions. Once into the main valley we were on a packed ski-doo trail and by dark had reached the Trans-Canada highway.

Centennial Year 1967 was special for the family. Our centennial project was to buy a new vehicle that had the capacity to accommodate everyone with their own place to sit and a seat belt.

Our choice was a GMC Carryall. We had never been to Vancouver Island so we planned a holiday to visit Long Beach, a place the Park Service was planning to start a new National Park. With a borrowed holiday trailer we travelled south to Montana, then west through Montana, Idaho and Washington states stopping at the Grand Coulee dam for a day. On to Seattle where we went to the top of the Needle. Catching a ferry we crossed over to the Olympic Peninsula and north to Port Angeles. We crossed the straits of Juan De Fuca on the ferry named the Coho to Victoria. Driving up the Island Highway we camped one night at Parksville with the tide very near our campsite. We were surprised the next morning to find the water about a half mile out, the family's first experience with ocean tides. On our way to Port Alberni we drove through MacMillan Park, amazed at the size of the fir trees. West of Port Alberni we were suddenly on a gravel logging road high above Sproat Lake. For three hours we travelled a mountain road more mountainous than any public road in the Rockies. A forest fire was burning on the Taylor River flats and we had to travel in convoy to Sutton Pass. The gravel road surface down Hydro hill was covered with loose boulders over which we bounced down to lower levels. We weren't sure it was such a good idea to have chosen this destination for our Centennial project. We made it to our destination, Greenpoint Campground, high above the ocean, with a vista overlooking miles of sandy beaches. The sights, sounds, smells and feeling of ocean fog and breezes were exhilarating. The kids and Edie didn't even stop to park the trailer but ran down the path. They scattered along the edge of the surf, shouting and looking at shells. David, the youngest, was like a Whirling Dervish running around in circles. It was hard getting them back up to the trailer to eat supper and go to bed.

For two weeks we explored between Tofino and Ucluelet and every day was an adventure we vividly remember. Every once in a while a moment of panic would come over me wondering if our truck would be able to pull the trailer back over the mountains. Our time ran out and sadly we headed for home. It had been a great holiday filled with fond memories of the Pacific Ocean. The smoky fires, playing in the surf, finding strange new creatures in tide pools and beach hikes would long be remembered. It would have been hard to believe that three years into the future, Ucluelet would be our new home.

In 1968, Pierre Trudeau ran a successful campaign and became Prime Minister. One of his platforms during his campaign was to streamline the Public Service. Each federal department was directed to develop a Management Services program and review the administrative and operational procedures of every function and make recommendations for improved efficiency.

The National Park Service was one function administered by the Department of Indian and Northern Affairs. One day in Banff, two senior departmental officers from Ottawa came into my office and told me I had been selected to serve on a Management Utilization Study Team, in short called a MUST team. This acronym in my opinion would certainly create an atmosphere of distrust when dealing with field managers.

I was curious to know why I was selected. The explanation was there were twenty departmental employees with a diversity of qualifications who were selected for their specific expertise in a certain function and mine was primarily for the Warden Service.

In detail, I was told I would be given a one-month's crash course in Organization and Methods in Ottawa and then be assigned to a two or three man team. Each team would be sent to the field over the next two years. As part of this team, I would be working in most of the National Parks and National Historic Parks west of Ottawa. For every three weeks in the field one week would be spent in Ottawa writing reports and making presentation to senior managers.

With the family remaining in Banff my visits home depended on the distance I would have to travel over a weekend. At the time of the program I was assured my position in Banff would be kept open.

CHAPTER

THE INFAMOUS 'MUST' PROGRAM
AND RETURN TO NATIONAL PARK

T HE terms of reference for the study team members explicitly stated that any recommendations must not be at the expense of staff lay-off. Scheduling, reassignment, improved equipment replacements, improved transportation, methods of communication, attrition, privatization and contracting were all valid reasons to be considered.

No manager welcomes anyone suggesting to him how to manage especially if he thinks it relates to cutbacks. Times were changing but many of the Chief Wardens had a very positive attitude towards old ways. Their personal experience had been survival in the back-country. Cutting fire wood, shovelling snow, looking after horses, cabin maintenance, telephone line maintenance and painting were all accepted activities and they could see no reason for change.

With the introduction of the public service union contracts and the trend towards job classification by function, a warden's classification by the bench mark method of evaluation would come out equal to a labourer. For some time I had an idea that the Warden Service could reorganize, rewrite their job description and take advantage of better methods of transportation and communication that were available. It could become more professional and leave maintenance responsibilities to people qualified to do that type of work.

I already had an indication this would be the way of the future from reading policy statements coming out of Ottawa, but the implementation would not necessarily be in the best interest of the Warden Service. One paper suggested the wardens could be classified as Security Officers.

Thinking over the offer to be part of the Study Team, I had

doubts any change recommended in the Warden Service to Chief Wardens who had the attitude, "this is the way it is and I can't see any reason for change," would be hard to convince them otherwise.

The other consideration was what about my family? I went home and talked it over with Edie. Could she handle the work looking after the family by herself most of the time? The easiest solution was to forget about the offer and just continue on in Banff. We were enjoying ourselves and the work was satisfying, but with her full support I agreed with the assignment.

The introductory one-month training program in Ottawa was intensive. Specialists from industry gave lectures on labour-management relations, time and motion techniques, contract administration, case studies of successful corporations, job classifications and management objectives. Time not spent in the classroom was utilized by reading assignments.

When the study team first visited a Park, an introductory meeting was held with the Superintendent and his senior staff and the ground rules discussed. In most instances a defensive position was taken by the Park managers, especially when part of the study included personal interviews with employees. The attitude of distrust overshadowed the opportunities that could be gained if compromises could be worked out. A smart manager could negotiate for better levels of classification, improved infrastructures for transportation and communication, manpower to meet rescheduling requirements of new union contracts and other advantages in exchange for updating the overall operation. Most opted to hold the line.

My interviews with individual wardens as I visited each park gave me an indication most were hoping for improvements. There were inconsistencies between parks on the duties of a Park Warden that could affect an individual's career opportunities. Job descriptions directly influences classification but not necessarily applied to the work a warden was actually assigned to do. It was common for highly skilled and qualified wardens to be in the same classification as a warden with limited ability. This situation was usually related to a Chief Warden's personal discretion.

In some parks the span of control a Chief Warden tried to exercise was too great for effective supervision. In a larger park a Chief Warden, additional to supervising about twenty wardens, was also responsible for telephone switchboard operators, a blacksmith, lookout observers, chainsaw operators, truck drivers, labour foremen, telephone linemen, timbermen and a stable boss.

The first recommendation was to relinquish all maintenance functions and transfer the positions to the Engineering arm of the

Park Service which were operating a duplicate function. This idea was strongly opposed in the firm belief Engineering did not appreciate the complexity of the Warden Service program.

The next recommendation, using Jasper as an example, was to divide the Park into six geographical units, referred to as Resource Management Areas. Concurrently, rewrite the wardens' job descriptions to emphasize the technical and management responsibilities relating to the complexity of managing and maintaining a resource area in keeping to the philosophy of National Parks.

Each area would be staffed with wardens classified at three levels. Level one would be the Area Manager. Level two, the technical, and level three the operational. This would give each area the independence to meet all normal Park requirements including back country patrols, search and rescue, public relations, law enforcement, game management and other related duties. The headquarters for each area would be located within the boundary of each district with vehicle access to Park Headquarters.

The six area managers would report to the Chief Warden who would then be reclassified as a Program Administrator. This change in organization would give a career warden the opportunity of four levels of promotion and still remain in the Resource Management program.

As basic as this concept was, managers gave only lip service to accepting this proposal and in turn deliberately implied to the wardens their world as they knew it was coming to an end. It may have appeared that way because the maintenance function was transferred to Engineering and very little effort was made to introduce wardens to their role as Resource managers. The old ways died hard and the image a warden had of himself living alone back in the mountains was being eroded. Many Chief Wardens had these memories and were not convinced change was necessary.

Over time some changes in classification have been introduced and recruitment for new members in the Warden Service require more professional and technical qualifications. The problem is the organizational structure has not kept pace with recruitment standards and many new wardens are not being utilized to their full potential. The more aggressive wardens soon moved on to other opportunities that offered a better future.

Out of curiosity, I checked with the National Parks personnel to see what was the current status (1991) of the Warden Service. Their classifications have been rewritten to General Technical but with no level that could be considered Resource Area Managers. The restructuring of the Warden Service organizational flow chart comparable to the recommendation of the Study Team's 1968 report is once again being considered.

At the completion of the Management Services study, I returned to my position in Banff to find many employees openly hostile towards me for my participation in recommending changes to the Parks operation. In discussion with some of the more outspoken individuals, especially in the Warden Service, I was surprised to learn they had not read any reports that were prepared at the conclusion of each Park study. The opinions expressed were based on hearsay and half-truths that had come down from managers trying to discredit recommendations which had been made to improve their operation. The fundamental problem was some managers were not capable of managing and were defending their position by making slanderous statements.

In the fall of 1969 I transferred to the Regional Office in Calgary into the position of Regional Visitor Services Officer and had to listen to the same criticism all over again. There were days when I wondered why I had put myself in such a position yet the experience was priceless. My farewell to Banff was to climb to the top of Mt. Rundle with Ron Langevin who was appointed my successor. In the same office building, Forestry Canada had their regional office and had been directed to the same task to review their operation, which they had ignored. After the study period was over, Ottawa arbitrarily cut forty of their positions without consultation. This sent a firm message that Ottawa was serious in trying to improve operations. Staff reduction in the Park Service was achieved by not filling positions considered redundant when they became vacant.

The past two years had been hectic, living out of a suitcase most of the time, so I decided to go on a two week fall hunting trip. Don Harford was the Assistant Superintendent of Banff and an avid hunter and I agreed to take him on a caribou hunt into the mountains north of Jasper. We made arrangements with Eddie Joachim living at Grande Cache to supply us with horses and to come with us into the Sulphur River area. I borrowed pack saddles and rigging we would need from Bud Brewster in Banff. When the gear and supplies were assembled we drove to Grande Cache and met Eddie. A two day trip and we were at a camp called Blue Grouse in the upper Sulphur River valley.

The weather was hot and the caribou were still bedded on the snowfields high on the mountains. After a couple of unsuccessful hunting days we finally spotted a large bull on the move across an open hillside high above us. Keeping out of sight and travelling parallel to him, we got ahead and waited until he came by. Don made an excellent shot and had himself an impressive trophy. We caped out the hide and butchered the meat and returned to camp.

Half way back to Grande Cache we camped and did some moose hunting for meat. While hunting along a trail we came to a dry gravel wash with willow brush growing up about six feet when all of a sudden I saw movement. It was a moose working his way towards us less than 100 yards away. Don got him in his scope but couldn't see exactly where he was aiming as the moose was so close the scope only showed hair. He fired and wounded the animal, who promptly charged us. I was packing my 30.30 Winchester with open sights and drew a bead between the eyes. The shot was good but his momentum carried him until he dropped almost at our feet.

There was more excitement the next day as we approached Grande Cache. We were travelling along with the pack outfit running loose when out of the timber came a wild stallion trying to take one of the mares away from the packstring. Eddie rushed to chase the stallion off and the stallion turned on him. Eddie was also riding a mare and the chase was on. His only protection was to ride into the heavy timber and the stallion turned his attention back to the pack outfit that by now was scattered all over the flats.

The next thing we saw was Eddie coming out of the timber carrying a pinepole lance and heading for the stallion, but the stallion was not about to leave. Eddie roped him, threw him down and tied up a hind leg. While the stallion was winded we got a pair of hobbles on his front feet and led him to Grande Cache where Eddie performed major surgery. Once he recovered he was added to Eddie's pack string. Don took his trophy to a taxidermist, had it wall-mounted and entered into the Alberta Fish and Game trophy competition. We were pleased to hear he had won the trophy award and went to the dinner when the presentation was made to him.

A winter in Calgary as a staff officer was not a position to get very excited about. Most of the work had to do with policy, statistics, budgets, five year plans, long term plans, and other intangibles that were never conclusive.

When the opportunity to move to Ucluelet with another staff officer and a naturalist to lay the ground work for a new National Park on the west coast of Vancouver Island, I was ready to go.

This move concluded my direct association with the Rocky Mountains and opened up a new world of management responsibilities. The experience prepared me for promotion to positions as a Superintendent of Point Pelee and Pukaskwa National Parks in Ontario and back to Vancouver Island as Superintendent of Pacific Rim National Park. As the family moved to different parts of Canada, the children completed their education and had an opportunity to select where they wanted to live and pursue careers of their choice.

The Camp family in 1970. Frank and Edie, Ross, Suzanne, John, Tom, Diane, Deborah and David.

EPILOGUE

Not mentioned by name but indirectly referred to in many instances in the book are Park Wardens Ross Baker, Chris Christiansen, Bill Essex, Gordon Gilroy, Clarence Shattuck, Harold Stack, Al Sturko, Bob Thompson, Max Winkler, Mac Elder and Chief Park Wardens Bob Hand and Glen Brooks.

INDEX